THE POETRY OF CRABBE

THE POETRY OF
CRABBE

Lilian Haddakin

1955

CHATTO & WINDUS

LONDON

Published by
Chatto & Windus Ltd
42 William IV Street
London W.C.2
∗
Clarke, Irwin & Co. Ltd
Toronto

CONTENTS

*

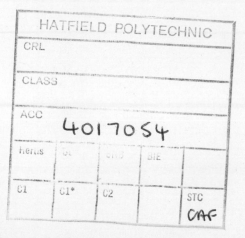

BIOGRAPHICAL TABLE

1754. George Crabbe born at Aldeburgh, Suffolk, 24 December.

c. 1762. Went to school at Bungay, Suffolk; the duration of his stay is uncertain.

1766. Went to school at Stowmarket, Suffolk, under Richard Haddon, a skilful mathematician.

1768. Apprenticed to an apothecary at Wickham Brook, near Bury St. Edmunds; wrote a good deal of verse during this apprenticeship.

1771. Went to a better situation with an apothecary at Woodbridge, Suffolk, where he remained for four years.

1772. Met his future wife, Sarah Elmy.

1775. Published *Inebriety, a Poem.* Returned to Aldeburgh during the summer, and spent some time as a labourer on Slaughden Quay. Set up practice as surgeon-apothecary by September of this year; studied botany and other branches of natural history during his leisure.

1776. Went to London towards the end of the year and remained there until about June 1777; lived in Whitechapel and tried to 'pick up a little surgical knowledge as cheaply as he could'.

1777. Returned to Aldeburgh to resume practice. Dangerously ill towards the end of this year.

1779. During the winter of 1779–80 decided to abandon unsuccessful practice and go to London to live by writing.

1780. Went to London in April, having secured a loan of five pounds. Witnessed the Gordon Riots in June. Unsuccessfully tried to secure the patronage of Lords North, Shelburne and Thurlow. *The Candidate, a Poetical Epistle* published in August.

1781. Appealed to Edmund Burke for help late in February or early in March. *The Library* published in July, with the help of Burke, with whom Crabbe stayed during the summer. Met Charles James Fox and Sir Joshua Reynolds later in the year. Ordained deacon in December.

1782. Returned to Aldeburgh as curate; he records that he preached his first sermon to 'unfriendly countenances'. Ordained priest in August. Appointed chaplain to the Duke of Rutland through Burke's influence; went to live at Belvoir Castle.

1783. Met Dr. Johnson during the winter of 1782–3. *The Village* published in May. Married Sarah Elmy in December; they had seven children, of whom only two survived to maturity—George, the poet's biographer, born 1785, and John, born 1787.

1785. Obtained curacy at Stathern, Leicestershire, where he lived for four years; acted as physician to the poor of the parish; studied botany and entomology during his leisure. *The Newspaper* published in March.

1787. His patron, the Duke of Rutland, died.

1789. Presented to livings of Muston, Leicestershire, and West Allington, Lincolnshire; held these livings for twenty-five years.

1792. Removed from Muston to Suffolk, where his wife had inherited property. During his residence in Leicestershire and Suffolk wrote and destroyed much verse and a treatise on botany.

1795. His account of the natural history of the Vale of Belvoir published in the first volume of Nichols's *The History and Antiquities of the County of Leicester.*

1801–2. Wrote three novels, which he destroyed.

1802. Began composition of *The Parish Register.*

1804. Began *The Borough.*

1805. Returned to Muston.

1806. *The Parish Register* completed and read in MS. to Charles James Fox.

1807. *Poems* published. The notable poems in this volume are *The Village, The Parish Register, The Library, The Newspaper, Sir Eustace Grey* and *The Hall of Justice.*

1810. *The Borough* published.

1812. *Tales in Verse* published.

1813. Mrs. Crabbe died. Crabbe dangerously ill.

1814. Became rector of Trowbridge, Wiltshire, where he lived for the rest of his life. Contracted an informal engagement with Charlotte Ridout, which was broken off after a few months.

Crabbe's geological studies belong chiefly to his years of residence in Wiltshire.

1817. Visited London, where he was mildly 'lionised', and met Thomas Campbell, Thomas Moore, Samuel Rogers and Sir George Beaumont. Also visited London in 1819 and several times during the eighteen-twenties; met Wordsworth and Southey.

1819. *Tales of the Hall* published.

1822. Visited Edinburgh, where he stayed with Sir Walter Scott; met Lockhart. Began to suffer from '*tic douloureux*' during this year.

1823. Seven-volume edition of Crabbe's poems published.

1831. Visited Bristol at time of riots.

1832. Died on 3 February.

1834. The first complete edition of his poems published by John Murray—*The Poetical Works of the Rev. George Crabbe: with his Letters and Journals, and his Life, by his Son.* 8 vols., octavo. The first volume consists of the *Life*; and the eighth, of the posthumous tales.

Note.—Quotations from Crabbe's poems and from the *Life* are taken from the edition of 1834. When necessary, line-references have been added from A. W. Ward's edition of Crabbe (3 vols., 1905–7).

INTRODUCTION

'M R. CRABBE is one of the most popular and admired of our living authors.' So Hazlitt wrote in 1825. That Crabbe's popularity was soon extinguished is not surprising. 'Pope in worsted stockings'—this unlucky epigram alone, in an age with no very high opinion of Pope himself, would suffice to discourage the general reader. Some admirers, indeed, were still to be found. Crabbe was acknowledged by Tennyson to have 'a world of his own'; Clough paid him the tribute of imitation; FitzGerald tirelessly canvassed his merits in letters to friends; Hardy received from his work his earliest impetus towards realism. But in print FitzGerald said little about his 'everlasting Crabbe', and the Victorian judgment is fairly represented by Leslie Stephen's somewhat patronising account of a narrator of homespun griefs in homespun verse.

Twentieth-century criticism, from Paul Elmer More to Dr. Leavis and Mr. Forster, has been more discriminating than Stephen's, but not much more vocal. While Crabbe has by now received adequate treatment from the biographers (his son's *Life* pictures the man vividly, if not altogether accurately, and Huchon presents him exhaustively, though not vividly[1]), he has had comparatively little critical attention. Francis

[1] *George Crabbe and his Times* (tr. Clarke, 1907). Huchon also treats Crabbe's work at great length, but with insufficient insight into his character as a poet. Alfred Ainger's *Crabbe* (1903) has less erudition but greater amenity.

Jeffrey's four notices in the *Edinburgh Review* still constitute the soundest sustained critical statement based on comprehensive study. Read without prejudice, Jeffrey remains helpful; yet he leaves many questions, which a twentieth-century reader would regard as important, not only unanswered but unasked. A different approach and a different method are needed if we are to see what Crabbe's achievement was.

The present study aims at showing what kind of satisfaction is to be gained from reading Crabbe, by pointing out the distinctive qualities of his work with the fulness of reference to the poems that is needed for illustration. It is, perhaps, not so much a matter of re-establishing the poet's reputation as of replacing the implicit and allusive or fragmentary by the explicit and comprehensive.

My concern is with the poems rather than with the man. I shall, however, begin with an account of the man. I do so not merely from an awareness that (in Walter Bagehot's words) 'people do not keep a tame steam-engine to write their books', nor with the intention of investigating closely the genesis of the poems, but because a knowledge of the man Crabbe—ironical, wry, vigilant, critical, compassionate, veracious (the relevant adjectives could be multiplied)—often helps in verifying an interpretation of the mood and tone of the poetry. It seems perverse to ignore the fairly ample evidence of this poet's sensibility that we possess. But the experiencing mind matters far more than the career; the more important details of the latter are given in a biographical table.

In treating the poems a purely chronological method is not the most fruitful. I hope to show how Crabbe's characteristic mode of writing evolved, examining his aims and assumptions and relating him to the poetic tradition to which he made his contribution. But it is more important to discover what constitutes the characteristic mode. This means asking, first, what is the 'poetry without an atmosphere' that Crabbe strove to write, or, what is 'actuality of relation'? And further, what sense of form had the poet, and how did he resolve the conflict between his earlier conception of form as design imposed upon amorphous subject-matter and his later sense of structure as elicited from material—material which was itself formative, as well as responsive to the poet's shaping? Finally, it is necessary to isolate those qualities in his work which have to do with the fact that he writes in verse; for he was not, as has sometimes been supposed, a short-story writer who rearranged his prose in lines of a certain length.

The greater part of this book, therefore, is devoted to a number of aspects of Crabbe's poetry which, together, make up his poetic mode. I shall not consider subject-matter in isolation from the way in which it is treated because, in the past, his social realism has been so heavily emphasised as almost to obscure the fact that what he had to say about people and things and places was given authentically poetic expression.

One or two incidental problems need mentioning. In some ways Crabbe is not easily manageable. What he could do best appears in his tales; but unwary critics treating too large a number of tales may become enmeshed in a web of summary and quotation and give, at best, cramped analyses of the structure of the tales or that of particular passages. The most satisfactory solution of this problem seems to be to choose a sufficient number of representative tales and passages for close consideration.[1] But there are two further difficulties in treating detached passages. As Jeffrey remarked, 'the pattern of [Crabbe's] arabesque is so large, that there is no getting a fair specimen of it without taking in a good space'; this, clearly, restricts the quoter's choice. Apart from this, many passages lose considerably by being removed from their context, for with Crabbe's work (as with that of poets whose repute as creators of closely articulated wholes stands higher than his) our response to the part is affected by our knowledge of what has preceded it and by our perception of what it is contributing to the poem as a whole. Nevertheless, something of the whole is contained in the fragment; and the detail of Crabbe's by no means homespun technique needs to be elucidated.

[1] Mr. Arthur Sale's article, 'The Development of Crabbe's Narrative Art' (*The Cambridge Journal*, May 1952, pp. 480-98), is a commendable step in this direction.

I

THE EXPERIENCING MIND

I

CRABBE's name has been so firmly associated with the notion of verbal photography that it may perhaps be doubted whether, as a writer, he possessed more sensibility than might be expected of a human camera. Yet any but a cursory reading of his poems will disclose a literary sensibility which is both powerful and individual. In his published work he is reticent about his purely personal feelings—the poetic tradition in which he grew up would encourage him to keep 'the mind which creates' distinct from 'the man who suffers'. But the two, however distinct, are related: the artist's sensibility which informs the poems is rooted in the experiencing mind of the man.

It is obvious that an account of Crabbe's personal fortunes, his professional career, his religious views, his moral code, his scientific pursuits, his affections, pleasures and anxieties, would scarcely constitute a picture of his sensibility; yet it embraces, or is fed by, all of these. In the present chapter I shall try to show the character of this sensibility, and to suggest the kind of modification it undergoes when it receives expression in the form of verse, using the evidence provided by the younger Crabbe's *Life* and by the autobiographical poem, *Infancy—A Fragment*.

We may as well begin, however, with a glance at the mythical Crabbe created by Hazlitt in *The Spirit of the*

15

Age. Hazlitt describes a literary sensibility of a kind. From his impression of the poems, added to the knowledge that the poet was a country clergyman, he tries to explain why certain qualities (chiefly qualities which repelled him) are, after all, only to be expected in the writings of such a man:

> The situation of a country clergyman is not necessarily favourable to the cultivation of the Muse. He is set down, perhaps, as he thinks, in a small curacy for life, and he takes his revenge by imprisoning the reader's imagination in luckless verse. Shut out from social converse, from learned colleges and halls, where he passed his youth, he has no cordial fellow-feeling with the unlettered manners of the *Village* or the *Borough*; and he describes his neighbours as more uncomfortable and discontented than himself. All this while he dedicates successive volumes to rising generations o noble patrons; and while he desolates a line of coast with sterile, blighting lines, the only leaf of his books where honour, beauty, worth, or pleasure bloom, is that inscribed to the Rutland family![1]

Crabbe's poetry, we are invited to believe, was the revenge he took on life for not treating him better. Life had, in fact, dealt with him much more harshly than his critic knew. He had not passed his youth in the comfort of 'learned colleges and halls'. The son of an impecunious collector of salt-duties at Aldeburgh, he had received an education inadequate to equip him for professional life, although his father gave him the best education he could afford. In his youth Crabbe was successively a surgeon's apprentice ('often employed in the drudgery of the farm', says the biographer, 'for his master had more occupations than one'), a warehouseman on Slaughden Quay, and (after a temporary improvement in his fortunes) an underfed country doctor.

[1] *The Spirit of the Age*, World's Classics ed. (1947), pp. 247-8.

It was necessity, he told his son, that drove him to be an author. And even after his year of semi-starvation in London, when he had 'arrived' as a poet and entered the Church through the friendly offices of Burke, he found himself for a time in the uncongenial situation of ducal chaplain.[1] The life of a country clergyman, when at length he obtained a living, proved far more favourable to the 'cultivation of the Muse'. If he had no cordial fellow-feeling with unlettered manners, he had a remarkably thorough knowledge of them at first-hand. His native line of coast, and the life of its inhabitants, *were* in great part desolate, sterile and blighted—and so he described them in *The Village*; his later poems amply repaired the omissions of this picture. But the notion of the noble savage evidently struck him as a foolish and fantastic paradox, for he took what practical steps he could to reduce the illiteracy and improve the manners; and in later life he devoted a substantial part of his stipend to almsgiving. As poet, clergyman and magistrate, he showed compassion devoid of sentimentality as well as a capacity for discriminating judgment.

Hazlitt was not alone in attributing to Crabbe a morose and querulous view of life, which was not in fact his. This misunderstanding is not unnatural, for the poet's acceptance of the facts of pain and human imperfection is thorough and, usually, calm. On the whole, he subscribed to Dr. Johnson's view of human life as 'a state in which much is to be endured and little enjoyed'. Like Johnson, he accepted this state partly

---

[1] A letter from Crabbe to Scott written in 1812 (*Life*, pp. 204-7) is by no means sycophantic in its references to the Duke of Rutland, the son of the poet's earlier patron; the tone is one of restrained asperity.

through rigorous self-discipline and partly through long familiarity with misfortune. He was much less easily disappointed and shocked than his critics: but this fact helped to determine the character of his wit and humour as well as that of his more sombre vein.[1]

The range and depth of Crabbe's keen, watchful sensibility are fairly well attested by what his son tells us about him. He was by nature swiftly responsive; this appeared abundantly in the affairs of daily life. We are told of an old lady (his wife's relation) who used to boast that she could 'screw Crabbe up and down like a fiddle'. This boast, says the poet's son, was not without reason, for he was 'at least as accessible to the slightest mark of kindness as to any species of offence'. He was accessible also to injuries inflicted on obscure strangers. Lockhart records an instance of this in a letter of reminiscence written to the biographer. Visiting Edinburgh in 1822, the poet was taken by Lockhart to see Holyrood House. He did not appear to care very much about the sight-seeing; but Lockhart adds:

I remember, however, that when the old dame who showed us Darnley's armour and boots complained of the impudence, as she called it, of a preceding visiter, who had discovered these articles to be relics of a much later age, your father warmly entered into her feelings; and said, as we came away, 'this pedantic puppyism was *inhumane*.'[2]

---

[1] It may be remarked that, although the tone of *Tales of the Hall* is more 'amiable and consoling' than that of *The Borough* or the earlier poems, this does not correspond with a change in the tenor of Crabbe's life. Thomas Campbell, who met him in 1817, told the poet's son: 'Though in a serene tone of spirits, he confessed to me that since the death of his wife he had scarcely known positive happiness' (*Life*, p. 244).

[2] *Ibid.* pp. 278-9.

Together with the firmest possible conviction of the supreme importance of conduct, Crabbe had an unusually active and acute moral sensibility which saw human actions, great or trivial, not only in relation to a religious or moral code (though this was also involved), but as indications of humane feeling or its lack. He constantly judged what he saw, but feeling accompanied judgment, and he was accustomed to consider the susceptibilities even of those whose behaviour he condemned. Hence came his dislike of personal satire:

> when the man you thus attack,
> And him expose with critic art,
> You put a creature to the rack—
> You wring, you agonise, his heart.[1]

It was from charity as well as from prudence that he took such pains to prevent the originals of his characters from being identified, as he explains in a letter to a friend:

I will tell you readily about my creatures, whom I endeavoured to paint as nearly as I could and dared; for, in some cases, I dared not. This you will readily admit: besides, charity bade me be cautious.[2]

Crabbe's over-sedulous care in this matter was noticed and ridiculed by the authors of *Rejected Addresses*, who manifestly had no such scruples themselves. *The Theatre*, their parody of Crabbe, has a preface in which the author is made to explain:

The animadversion I have thought it right to make on the noise created by tuning the orchestra, will, I hope, give no lasting remorse to any of the gentlemen employed in the band. It is to be

---

[1] *Satire* (*Works*, IV, p. 110).
[2] *Life*, p. 232 (letter to Mary Leadbeater, 1 December 1816).

desired that they would keep their instruments ready tuned, and strike off at once. . . .

> '—One fiddle will
> Give, half-ashamed, a tiny flourish still,'

was originally written 'one hautboy will;' but, having providentially been informed, when this poem was upon the point of being sent off, that there is but one hautboy in the band, I averted the storm of popular and managerial indignation from the head of its blower: as it now stands, 'one fiddle' among many, the faulty individual will, I hope, escape detection.[1]

The poet, not surprisingly, found that there was a little 'undeserved ill-nature' in this preface, but it is pleasant to record that he enjoyed the parody of his verse.

Even in his dreams, this moral sensibility appears to have operated constantly and painfully. In a journal kept during his visit to London in the summer of 1817 he records that he has been 'incommoded by dreams, such as would cure vanity for a time in any mind where they could gain admission'. It is clear that what distressed him most were the images of degradation:

Awake, I had been with the high, the apparently happy: we were very pleasantly engaged, and my last thoughts were cheerful. Asleep, all was misery and degradation, not my own only, but of those who had been.—That horrible image of servility and baseness—that mercenary and commercial manner! It is the work of imagination, I suppose; but it is very strange.[2]

What could not be enjoyed (and he found much that could) had to be endured. His religion furnished him

---

[1] James and Horace Smith, *Rejected Addresses*, ed. Boyle (1929), p. 109.

[2] *Life*, p. 253. A more detailed account of the same experience, or a very similar one, is given in his poem, *The World of Dreams*, stanzas xxxiii-xxxv (*Works*, IV, p. 127).

with a rule of moral life—this appears always to have been its chief value to him. His son describes the religious outlook which had been inculcated by the poet's mother:

she was . . . a deeply devout woman; but her seriousness was not of the kind that now almost exclusively receives that designation. Among persons of her class, at least, at that period, there was a general impression that the doctrinal creed ought rather to be considered the affair of the pastor than of the humble and unlearned members of his flock—that the former would be held responsible for the tenets he inculcated—the latter for the practical observance of those rules of conduct and temper which good men of all persuasions alike advocate and desire to exemplify.[1]

According to this view, misfortunes were a spur to self-amendment and the more diligent performance of duty. In his son's opinion, Crabbe's own attitude is represented by that of the clergyman in *Tales of the Hall*, whom some of his parishioners censure as a mere 'moral teacher'. He strongly disliked religious enthusiasm, for the notion that the individual was accorded a considerable measure of personal attention, celestial or infernal, seemed to him to be closely associated with spiritual arrogance or vanity.[2] The efficacy of his own

[1] *Ibid.* pp. 105-6.

[2] His objections to the Calvinist and Arminian doctrines are, to a great extent, practical—he thinks the former likely to drive people to despair, and the latter likely to encourage slackness in the performance of practical duties. His attitude towards religious enthusiasm, and its grounds, may be studied in *The Borough*, Letter IV (*Sects and Professions in Religion*), Letter XIX (*The Parish Clerk*), Letter XXI (*Abel Keene*); *Tales in Verse*, XV (*The 'Squire and the Priest*), XIX (*The Convert*). His own view is that religion has a rational basis and that, although there are doubts, 'if we wait until all doubts be cleared away, we shall die doubting'. He also adduces arguments bearing on the respectability and utility of Christianity—'a religion which has satisfied

unenthusiastic religion as a source of moral strength in adversity is well illustrated by a remark in the journal he kept during his stay in London in 1780:

We are helped, I'm persuaded, with spirits in our necessities. I did not, nor could not, conceive that, with a very uncertain prospect before me, a very bleak one behind, and a *very* poor one around me, I should be so happy a fellow.[1]

He was convinced that there existed in each human being a certain core of personal integrity which was indestructible by outward circumstances, though vulnerable from within. Its indestructibility by circumstances is the theme of *Ellen Orford* (*The Borough*, Letter XX); the fear of its vulnerability in other ways is evident in the passage on his dreams already quoted.

So far I have dwelt chiefly on the more sombre and solemn aspects of Crabbe; but, after all, they represent what is most immediately striking in him. It remains to record various sources of satisfaction on which he drew and which all contributed in some degree to his poetry.

There was, first of all, the satisfaction of contemplating and studying the external world. Lest it should be thought that Crabbe looked upon the external world only as a repository of specimens to be collected and classified, it may be as well to refer to two passages in the *Life* which show that, on the contrary, his response to natural phenomena was powerful and lively. The

the wisest, converted the most wicked, and consoled the most afflicted of our fellow-creatures' (Huchon, *op. cit.* p. 214). He was occasionally accessible to the non-rational in religion; sometimes reluctantly. He is half inclined to attribute the bad dreams referred to above to 'mortifying spirits', but says: 'I would not appear to myself superstitious' (*Life*, p. 253).

[1] *Ibid.* p. 64.

more striking of the two passages is a description, based on Mrs. Crabbe's recollection of the incident, of his demeanour on seeing the 'great and memorable meteor' which appeared in 1783:

. . . my mother and he were returning, in the evening, over a wide open common near Beccles. It was late, dull, and cloudy: n an instant the dark mass opened just in front of them. The clouds were rolled back like a scroll; and the glorious pheno-menon burst forth as large as the moon, but infinitely more brilliant; majestically sailed across the heavens, varying its form every instant, and, as it were, unfolding its substance in suc-cessive sheaths of fire, and scattering lesser meteors, as it moved along. My mother, who happened to be riding behind, said that, even at that awful moment (for she concluded that the end of all things was at hand), she was irresistibly struck with my father's attitude. He had raised himself from his horse, lifted his arm, and spread his hand towards the object of admiration and terror, and appeared transfixed with astonishment.[1]

This was a rare phenomenon. But elements of the visible world with which he had been familiar all his life were capable of exerting a very strong attraction.

It was, I think [says the poet's son], in the summer of 1787, that my father was seized, one fine summer's day, with so intense a longing to see the sea, from which he had never before been so long absent, that he mounted his horse, rode alone to the coast of Lincolnshire, sixty miles from his house, dipped in the

[1] *Ibid.* pp. 123-4. Sir Eustace Grey's hallucinations of the 'nimble beams of brilliant light' may have originated in Crabbe's seeing the meteor, his memory of the sight, possibly, being incorporated in an opium dream. He began to take opium on medical advice in or about 1790, and continued to take 'a constant but slightly increasing dose' thereafter (*Life*, p. 161). On supernormal awareness of bright light or colour as a characteristic of opium dreams, see M. H. Abrams, *The Milk of Paradise: The Effect of Opium Visions on the Works of De Quincey, Crabbe, Francis Thompson and Coleridge* (1934), p. 20.

waves that washed the beach of Aldborough, and returned to Stathern.[1]

Crabbe pursued the study of natural history, in the first place, to take his mind off his own anxieties. As an unsuccessful country doctor, he was 'glad to relieve his mind by fixing it on the herbs that grew on the wayside'.[2] A few years later the ducal chaplain found solace from occasions of 'more than usual ceremony, or more abundant conviviality' in 'wandering through the deep glades and secluded paths of the woods, catching beetles, moths, butterflies, and collecting mosses, lichens, or other botanical specimens'.[3] Later still, botany mingled with domestic pleasures, such as excursions with his family:

Sometimes, as we proceeded, my father read aloud; sometimes he left us for a while to botanise among the hedgerows, and returned with some unsightly weed or bunch of moss, to him precious.[4]

He studied botany with 'insatiable ardour'. He wrote a great part of an Essay on Botany in English, but left it unfinished because of the remonstrance of a Mr. Davies of Trinity College, Cambridge, a man who, 'though little tinged with academical peculiarities, could not stomach the notion of degrading such a science by treating of it in a modern language'.[5]

The poet's son comments on the variety, zeal and untidiness of his studies in natural history:

There was, perhaps, no one of its departments to which he did not, at some time or other, turn with peculiar ardour; but, generally speaking, I should be inclined to say, that those usually

<hr />

[1] *Life*, p. 135.   [2] *Ibid.* p. 44.   [3] *Ibid.* p. 115.
[4] *Ibid.* pp. 141-2.   [5] *Ibid.* p. 134.

considered as the least inviting had the highest attractions for him. In botany, grasses, the most useful, but the least ornamental, were his favourites; in minerals, the earths and sands; in entomology, the minuter insects. His devotion to these pursuits appeared to proceed purely from the love of science and the increase of knowledge—at all events, he never seemed to be captivated with the mere beauty of natural objects, or even to catch any taste for the arrangement of his own specimens.[1]

Among the pursuits of his leisure was a more usual concern of poets, the reading of poetry. He was well read in the English poets, had a 'strong partiality for Latin poetry', and also learnt to read French and Italian. Horace was his favourite among the Roman poets; among the English, Chaucer, Shakespeare, Samuel Butler, Dryden and Pope. He was, moreover, a great novel-reader and 'seldom passed a day without reading part of some such work, and was never very select in the choice of them'. (Lest we should think the poet frivolous in his tastes, the biographer tells us that 'even from the most trite of these fictions, he could sometimes catch a train of ideas that was turned to excellent use'.[2]) He himself wrote three novels, which he burnt. He was also a skilful mathematician. According to his son, he had 'no real love for painting, or music, or architecture, or for what a painter's eye considers as the beauties of landscape', though in fact his poetry reveals some appreciation of both painting and landscape.

But the study of human nature had a far stronger hold on Crabbe than the study of literature or external

---

[1] *Ibid.* pp. 164-5. Nevertheless, the poet's account of the natural history of the Vale of Belvoir shows a certain feeling for 'beautiful insects'.

[2] *Ibid.* p. 158.

nature. He said 'he preferred walking in the streets, and observing the passers-by, to the finest natural scene'. And just as he preferred to study grasses rather than flowers, so he seems to have taken a deeper interest in the sombre or humdrum parts of the human scene than in the august spectacles which it occasionally provided. Thus, his visit to Edinburgh in 1822 coinciding with that of George IV, he attended a levee; but his inclinations evidently drew him elsewhere—he rambled among the 'obscurest wynds and closes' of the Old Town, and 'repeated his visits several times to the Royal Infirmary of Edinburgh, and expressed great admiration of the manner in which the patients were treated. He also examined pretty minutely the interior of the Bedlam.'[1]

The science of the human mind, his son assures us, was his chief passion. But it was more than a science. He may be said to have regarded life, at least intermittently, as material for his art. The journal he kept during his visit to London in 1817 contains the following entry:

July 4th.—Morning view, and walk with Mr. Heber and Mr. Stanhope. Afterwards Mr. Rogers, Lady S., Lady H. A good picture, if I dare draw it accurately: to place in lower life, would lose the peculiarities which depend upon their station; yet, in any station.[2]

These words would have caused some misgivings in the minds of the many acquaintances who were so agreeably impressed (and surprised) by the mildness of manner which the author of The Borough displayed. Thomas Campbell was exceptional in perceiving that

[1] Life, p. 278. The biographer is quoting from Lockhart's letter.
[2] Ibid. p. 246.

the amiable cleric possessed 'a vigilant shrewdness that almost eluded you by keeping its watch so quietly'.[1]

The study of human nature was not, like the study of plants, insects and rocks, immediately conducive to calm of mind. Sometimes, it is true, Crabbe recorded with considerable detachment events which he had just witnessed, as in the account of the Gordon Riots in his London journal of 1780. At other times he was deeply moved by what he saw. This was so when he visited a condemned felon in Newgate; and when, about a quarter of a century later, he set himself to describe what he had seen, he was 'much affected'. But emotion had not caused his vigilance to relax; he had been able to discern in the felon's expression the ruling passion of despair, with which those fainter passions which he had at first expected to see (shame, resentment or hope or fear) could not co-exist. The act of concentrating his faculties on what he was observing, in order to grasp the truth as firmly and fully as possible, seems to have transmuted his own feelings. And—at least in his writings—he appears capable of entering into the experience of his characters to such a degree that he achieves complete forgetfulness of himself and of everything except the object on which his mental eye is fixed. On the readiness and liveliness of his sympathy in personal intercourse, the biographer quotes the testimony of a friend of Crabbe's:

. . . from his knowledge of human nature, he was able, in a re-markable manner, to throw himself into the circumstances of those who needed his help—*no sympathy was like his*; and no man, perhaps, had the inmost feelings of others more frequently laid open to his inspection.[2]

---

[1] *Ibid.* p. 244.
[2] *Ibid.* pp. 259-60. The italics are not mine.

But the study of human nature was also a source of much entertainment. This was so even when the object of study caused the observer some discomfort. It is evident from the *Life* that Mrs. Crabbe's aunt, Mrs. Tovell, was a loquacious and overbearing scold; but she was a fine specimen of her type, and Crabbe appreciated her as a 'character'. She is rendered, in essentials, with caustic brilliance in the sketch of the Widow Goe in *The Parish Register*. The poet is capable, too, of ironical wit as he recounts his own experiences. He visits Holyrood House:

We went into the little room where the Queen and Rizzio sat, when his murderers broke in and cut him down as he struggled to escape: they show certain stains on the floor; and I see no reason why you should not believe them made by his blood, if you can.[1]

Or he describes his situation and pastimes for the information of a friend in Ireland (a literal-minded person, as it happened, whom the ironical tone eluded):

Am I not a great fat Rector, living upon a mighty income, while my poor curate starves with six hungry children, upon the scraps that fall from the luxurious table? Do I not visit that horrible London, and enter into its abominable dissipations? Am I not this day going to dine on venison and drink claret? Have I not been at election dinners, and joined the Babel-confusion of a town-hall? Child of simplicity! am I fit to be a friend to you?[2]

He seems also to have had a nice sense of the irony of situation, if we may judge from an incident related by one of his friends in a letter to the biographer. Crabbe was travelling in a stage-coach from Bath with a local

[1] *Life*, p. 274.   [2] *Ibid*. pp. 257-8.

squire who was ignorant of his companion's identity; and

as they approached Calne, the squire mentioned the names of certain poets of the neighbourhood; expressed his admiration of your father's earlier works;—but ventured to hint that one of the latter, I forget which, was a failure, and that he would do well to lay his pen aside. 'Sir,' said your father, 'I am quite of your opinion. Artists and poets of all ages have fallen into the same error. Time creeps on so gently, that they never find out that they are growing old!'[1]

'The squire, perhaps, was right,' said Crabbe later, 'but you know I was an incompetent judge upon that subject.' He was a shrewd enough judge of the sentiments of the reading public, however. Announcing to his son that he has left enough tales in manuscript to make up a posthumous volume, he is grimly confident of their success, for 'the works of authors departed are generally received with some favour, partly as they are old acquaintances, and in part because there can be no more of them'.[2]

Among the chief pleasures of Crabbe's life must certainly be reckoned the activity of composing poetry. It was his habit to compose while he was doing something with his hands:

While searching for and examining plants or insects, he was moulding verses into measure and smoothness. No one who observed him at these times could doubt that he enjoyed exquisite pleasure in composing. He had a degree of action while thus walking and versifying, which I hardly ever observed when he was preaching or reading. The hand was moved up and down;

[1] *Ibid.* p. 303.   [2] *Ibid.* p. 311.

the pace quickened. He was, nevertheless, fond of considering poetical composition as a species of task and labour, and would say, 'I have been hard at work, and have had a good morning.'[1]

He was able to forget immediate distractions while composing. He records in his journal for 23 July 1817:

A vile engagement to an oratorio at church, by I know not how many noisy people; women as well as men. Luckily, I sat where I could write unobserved, and wrote forty lines, only interrupted by a song of Mrs. Brand—a hymn, I believe. It was less doleful than the rest.[2]

Of the years 1817–18, when he was finishing *Tales of the Hall*, his son tells us:

His notebook was at this time ever with him in his walks, and he would now and then lay down his hammer to insert a new or amended couplet. He fancied that autumn was, on the whole, the most favourable season for him in the composition of poetry; but there was something in the effect of a sudden fall of snow that appeared to stimulate him in a very extraordinary manner. It was during a great snow storm that, shut up in his room, he wrote almost *currente calamo* his Sir Eustace Grey.[3]

He was not often much moved emotionally as he wrote. *Sir Eustace Grey* is an exception—the only other recorded exceptions are the lines on the condemned felon in the twenty-third Letter of *The Borough*, and the somewhat doubtful case of some stanzas written in 1780 which moved their author when he read them very soon after their composition:

---

[1] *Life*, p. 164; the biographer is quoting from a memorandum supplied by his brother.
[2] *Ibid.* pp. 254-5.   [3] *Ibid.* p. 262.

For the first time in my life that I recollect, I have written three or four stanzas that so far touched me in the reading them, as to take off the consideration that they were things of my own fancy.[1]

Usually, however, he worked steadily, and without 'transport'. He himself tells us very little about the experience of composition. In the journal of 1817 he often makes a note of the number of lines he has written (he tries to maintain a stint of thirty lines a day), but seldom even alludes to the subject of the poem. And yet, though the tone of much of his poetry suggests that he wrote as one consciously practising a craft, he found that poetry could sometimes be composed without the help of the conscious mind.

I recollect [says Lockhart, referring to Crabbe's Scottish visit] that he used to have a lamp and writing materials placed by his bedside every night; and when Lady Scott told him she wondered the day was not enough for authorship, he answered, 'Dear Lady, I should have lost many a good hit, had I not set down, at once, things which occurred to me in my dreams.'[2]

This passage will bear more than one interpretation; but the phrase 'many a good hit' seems to me to refer to the efficient, if fragmentary, expression of what he had to say rather than to the other material which his dreams sometimes gave him. If the 'good hits' were suitable for use more or less as they were dreamt, the stuff of his dreams needed to be arranged or worked up in some way. Even *The World of Dreams* is clearly neither a 'dreamt poem' like *Kubla Khan* nor a record of one particular dream just as it occurred, but an account of a representative dream. In the hallucinations of Sir Eustace Grey the dream-images are elaborated

[1] *Ibid.* p. 65.   [2] *Ibid.* p. 280.

with some care—they are *composed* into poetry suitable to be offered to the public. And even so, Crabbe's estimate of these dream-images as 'the mind's delusion' is evident in the superscription of the poem: '*Scene—A Madhouse*.'[1]

II

We know that the characters in Crabbe's poems had their originals, but were modified versions of these originals, presented in altered circumstances and situations. Correspondingly, the literary sensibility revealed in the poems is rooted in Crabbe's sensibility as a man. But it functions differently, and it functions selectively. If we know both the *Life* and the *Poetical Works* we can recognise the man in the author and the author in the man. Yet the relation between the poetic sensibility and the experiencing mind cannot be stated in simple terms. Despite a good many lapses, Crabbe had too much literary tact to make his poetry a vehicle for expressing all his interests and feelings indiscriminately. It was not just that he refrained from writing on 'the great subjects of religion' because he found that he personally could not write religious poetry that satisfied him. It was also that he perceived that poetry and, say, natural history should not be yoked by violence together. Occasionally we may find in his work phrases that recall the poetic style of Erasmus Darwin; but it was certainly

[1] A distinction has to be drawn between the use of his dream-experiences which Crabbe makes in *Sir Eustace Grey* and that which he makes at the end of the felon's dream (*The Borough*, Letter XXIII); the shock of waking from pleasant dream to unpleasant reality which is so forcibly conveyed is, after all, a common experience, though it is intensified by its context here.

no part of Crabbe's programme (as it was of Darwin's) to lure his readers to the study of botany by means of the pleasures of poetry. Botanical terms may appear in the footnotes, but when, for some special purpose, they appear in the verse (and they do so very rarely) their lack of 'poeticality' is always emphasised. Crabbe resembles Wordsworth in striving to give 'immediate pleasure to a human Being possessed of that information which may be expected from him, not as a lawyer, a physician, a mariner, an astronomer, or a natural philosopher, but as a Man'.[1]

His scientific studies certainly affected his poetry, but they did so in an indirect way. It may perhaps be said that they affected the pre-history of the poems. They trained the author's powers of observation and analysis; and it can hardly be doubted that they helped to make him dissatisfied with generalities and caused him, in making use of his observations, to work from the individual to the general instead of the other way round, to distinguish the accidental from the essential, and to trace common characteristics in partially dissimilar, but related, beings.[2] Occasionally, too, they caused him to see the contemporary scene, or even the human race in general, from an unusual angle. Fossils made him view mankind momentarily as an insignificant and repulsive kind of worm:

> It is a lovely place, and at the side
> Rises a mountain-rock in rugged pride;

---

[1] Preface to the second edition of *Lyrical Ballads*.

[2] The critic who reviewed *The Village* in *The Monthly Review* in 1783 complains that Crabbe has reversed 'that indispensable rule, which both painters and poets should equally attend to . . . namely, to form their individuals from ideas of general nature'.

And in that rock are shapes of shells, and forms
Of creatures in old worlds, of nameless worms,
Whose generations lived and died ere man,
A worm of other class, to crawl began.[1]

Crabbe was not always so successful in incorporating scientific knowledge in his poetry. A curious but not uninstructive example of the naturalist guiding the poet is to be found in the second Letter of *The Borough*, where Crabbe admonishes the artist who tries to make new walls look venerable by painting imitation lichens on them:

In three short hours shall thy presuming hand
Th' effect of three slow centuries command?
Thou may'st thy various greens and greys contrive,
They are not Lichens, nor like aught alive.[2]

The naturalist winces; the poet makes a complaint on his behalf. But the result is poetically trivial.

It is, incidentally, worth recording Crabbe's pedantic but suggestive note on these lines:

If it should be objected, that centuries are not slower than hours, because the speed of time must be uniform, I would answer, that I understand so much, and mean that they are slower in no other sense, than because they are not finished so soon.

'The speed of time must be uniform.' He did, indeed, understand so much. Yet few writers have exploited so brilliantly, and in such a variety of ways, a perception of the differences in the speed at which time *seems* to

[1] *Tales of the Hall*, XIII; *Works*, VII, p. 43. Reviewing this work, Jeffrey merely notes the passage as being 'in Mr. Crabbe's best style of concise and minute description'; its bearing on the question of the age of the world appears to have escaped him.
[2] *Works*, III, p. 35.

pass—or, to revert to the poet's dreams, an awareness of how time can appear to stand still, as it does in *Sir Eustace Grey*.

III

Crabbe's autobiographical poem, *Infancy*, written in 1816, is a valuable document.[1] It not only tells us something about the author's sensibility, but also shows how this sensibility operates when Crabbe is expressing himself in verse; the metre used, the heroic couplet, had been his staple metre for half a century. In this poem he comes nearer than in anything else he wrote to giving us a record of a few minutes of his consciousness: a train of mingled reflection, emotion and reminiscence.

The lines are the expression of a sombre mood, not the formulation of a conviction that life is predominantly painful: the poet does not merely assent to the notion, he feels its truth as he writes. Unlike the verse he published, this fragment is essentially a private affair arising immediately out of the poet's distress, which ebbs and flows while he is engaged in thinking and remembering. Because the poem isolates this distress, the impression of Crabbe's outlook on life which we receive from it cannot be said to correspond to that which is made by his published work as a whole, where the pleasant, or at least the unpainful, often engages our attention.

But it is significant that even this private effusion of grief should be, not *Lines Written in Dejection*, but *Infancy*. Crabbe has provided himself with a definite

[1] The MS. is dated 16 April 1816 (Huchon, *op. cit.* p. 7, n. 3). The poem is given in *Works*, IV, pp. 101-6.

topic to reflect upon: What can memory tell us about
our infancy?

> Who on the new-born light can back return,
> And the first efforts of the soul discern—
> Waked by some sweet maternal smile, no more
> To sleep so long or fondly as before?

Crabbe's recollections of early childhood furnished
him with no intimations of immortality. It is unlikely
that he ever speculated on the possibility that they
might do so; he had not a speculative mind. But he
entertains something like Wordsworth's notion that the
child is father of the man, though he is led to this view
by a recurrent *sinking* of the heart:

> looking back as early as I can,
> I see the griefs that seize their subject Man,
> That in the weeping Child their early reign began.

Wordsworth's mode of apprehending life, as embodied
in the *Immortality Ode*, is alien to Crabbe. He never
draws upon 'shadowy recollections' as a source of anything he would call knowledge; but knowledge is what
he wants. He does not question 'sense and outward
things'; but he does ask questions, in this poem and
elsewhere, about the capacities of the human mind.
Scrutinising his own recollections of infancy, he em-
phatically denies that memory extends as far back as
the 'awakening' of the soul:

> No! Memory cannot reach, with all her power,
> To that new birth, that life-awakening hour.
> No! all the traces of her first employ
> Are keen perceptions of the senses' joy,
> And their distaste.

All we learnt reliably from our earliest perceptions was 'That figs were luscious, and that rods had smart'. There is nothing mysterious here, and nothing of great consequence. In any case, Crabbe reminds himself, we must bear in mind that memory can make mistakes; she

> encounters, in the doubtful view,
> With imperfection and distortion too.

We must remember the shortcomings of our mental faculties, yet we must use these faculties. Surely, he suggests, we can at least ask memory whether good or evil is more abundant (in this poem 'good' means 'pleasure' and 'evil' means 'pain'). The answer memory gives us is unequivocal: without pain, there could be no pleasure:

> Alas! and what is earthly good? 't is lent
> Evil to hide, to soften, to prevent,
> By scenes and shows that cheat the wandering eye,
> While the more pompous misery passes by;
> Shifts and amusements that awhile succeed,
> And heads are turn'd, that bosoms may not bleed.

Pleasures are merely the sideshows which distract our attention for a short time from the main spectacle. The making of this metaphor may well have served Crabbe as a sideshow, momentarily relieving the pressure of dejection. It has certainly caused him to postpone saying in a direct manner what he thinks about pleasure and pain. He now proceeds to make a statement which does, indeed, employ figurative language, but employs it very sparingly, and in a different way, physical pain being taken to typify pain of any kind:

> For what is Pleasure, that we toil to gain?
> 'T is but the slow or rapid flight of Pain.

> Set Pleasure by, and there would yet remain,
> For every nerve and sense the sting of Pain:
> Set Pain aside, and fear no more the sting,
> And whence your hopes and pleasures can ye bring?
> No! There is not a joy beneath the skies,
> That from no grief nor trouble shall arise.

At this point another sideshow is provided. The poet illustrates the truth of what he has said by referring to ordinary life: the lover enjoys his mistress's smile, but this is because it alone can relieve the pain caused by her absence. If we look at his married life we shall see that this is so:

> For, married, soon at will he comes and goes;
> Then pleasures die, and pains become repose,
> And he has none of these, and therefore none of those.

The sketch of the lover is a description of a specimen of common human experience. But Crabbe is, after all, concerned with his own personal predicament, and it is not by examining specimens of the average experience that he is able to deal with this predicament.

The poem now becomes explicitly autobiographical —Crabbe is his own specimen. He now takes a foreshortened view of his life, in which the child is seen as the father of the man; but this view, again, is interrupted by a series of similes which help to express further generalisations about joy and grief; next, he alludes to the typical pleasures of his childhood in connection with what has so far been his main contention: that pleasure is relief from pain:

> Yes! looking back as early as I can,
> I see the griefs that seize their subject Man,
> That in the weeping Child their early reign began:

Yes! though Pain softens, and is absent since,
He still controls me like my lawful prince.
Joys I remember, like phosphoric light
Or squibs and crackers on a gala night.
Joys are like oil; if thrown upon the tide
Of flowing life, they mix not, nor subside:
Griefs are like waters on the river thrown,
They mix entirely, and become its own.
Of all the good that grew of early date,
I can but parts and incidents relate:
A guest arriving, or a borrow'd day
From school, or schoolboy triumph at some play:
And these from Pain may be deduced; for these
Removed some ill, and hence their power to please.

The similes in the middle lines, though apt enough, are contrived. The poet appears once more to have sought a temporary escape from feeling in the exercise of ingenuity and in the imitation of his admired predecessor Pope.[1]

The idea that the child is father of the man now assumes greater importance; the remainder of the poem is devoted to showing how early experiences prefigured later ones. Crabbe brings himself to contemplate a particular experience: his 'first-born ill', the death of an infant sister. He observes that the very strangeness and

[1] The couplet, 'Joys are like oil . . .' recalls 'Words are like leaves; and where they most abound,/Much fruit of sense beneath is rarely found'. Crabbe's similes are often of this 'detachable' kind. Jeffrey remarked that they 'are almost all elaborate and ingenious, and rather seem to be furnished from the efforts of a fanciful mind, than to be exhaled by the spontaneous ferment of a heated imagination'. (*Essays on English Poets and Poetry: from 'The Edinburgh Review'*, 'The New Universal Library', n.d., p. 360.) On reading this, Crabbe said: 'Jeffrey is quite right: my usual method has been to think of such illustrations, and insert them *after finishing a tale*'. (*Works*, VI, p. 36, n. 2.)

novelty of the emotion he then felt have fixed it firmly in his memory. (Curiously enough, his memory of the event which gave rise to the emotion was indistinct— the Aldeburgh parish register shows that the 'infant sister' of the poem was really an infant brother.[1]) But since then he has been more deeply distressed by other deaths—his mother's and (more recently) his wife's— and as he recalls these his unhappiness reaches its climax. His utterance becomes hesitant and disjointed. He dare not try to set down what he feels, and is aware of the faintness and inadequacy of words. He seeks refuge now in deliberate and minute reminiscence:

> But here I dwell not—let me, while I can,
> Go to the Child, and lose the suffering Man.

He goes, not to childhood in general, but to a particular incident—his 'first-born joy', a boating expedition. There follows a miniature tale in verse, written in a manner much like that of the tales he was composing at this time for publication. The poet does not seek to recreate the experience of the child: the emotions and events of which he writes are drawn from the memory and looked at with the attentive mental eye of the adult. And although his purpose in relating the incident is to show how the feelings he experienced as a child followed a pattern which has often been repeated, his description of the expedition has a generous alloy of hard and particularised physical fact; it has also a generalisation about the tastes of children (that they like joining in the activities of adults better than playing their own games), an explanation of the extraordinarily intense and unmixed pleasure which children are capable of

---

[1] Huchon, *op. cit.* p. 7, n. 3.

feeling, and a careful account of the successive stages of intoxication. Now material of this kind is what we should expect to find in any of Crabbe's tales, whether or not the theme of the tale had any reference to himself personally. Moreover, in this personal tale, while Crabbe remembers his feelings with great distinctness, he has sufficient detachment, viewing them across half a century, to be able to set down his impressions of the day with no less regard for truth to nature over his emotions than over externals. The poetic process in this case is scarcely emotion recollected in tranquillity; it is emotion recollected in order to achieve tranquillity by means of a total concentration of the mind on something other than the poet's present self. To Crabbe, collectedness of mind (implying the control, not the absence, of feeling) was a desirable state in itself. It was also necessary for the composition of poetry, and it appears from this autobiographical fragment that the very activity of composition contributed to collectedness of mind, and may therefore be said to have modified Crabbe's total sensibility.

The child's joy on setting out is presented succinctly; Crabbe does not 'write up' the rapture. But in a few lines a certain luminosity appears, which is not to be interpreted as a 'visionary gleam', but as a record of emotion actually felt:

> The linnet chirp'd upon the furze as well,
> To my young sense, as sings the nightingale.
> Without was paradise—because within
> Was a keen relish, without taint of sin.

Crabbe explains and judges the emotion. He is aware that his young sense improved the actual world; he is sure that the nightingale really sings better than the linnet. He knows that the external world is not at all paradisal, and that what made it seem so was his own gusto. The keen relish, he implies, is soon dispelled by the taint of sin, the expulsion from Eden being repeated in each human life.

The short duration of his happiness on this particular day is not, however, a result of his own misdeeds. The party lands; the child wanders off and loses his way in the town. When he rejoins his companions the day is already spoilt:

> Mid-day it was, and, as the sun declined,
> The good, found early, I no more could find.

The men drink and grow bad-tempered; after they have all re-embarked,

> The lads play'd idly with the helm and oar,
> And nervous women would be set on shore,
> Till 'civil dudgeon' grew, and peace would shine no more.

This is the only point in the whole poem capable of providing the slightest outlet for Crabbe's sardonic astringency. It makes a brief and oblique appearance—the phrase 'civil dudgeon' is from the opening couplet of *Hudibras*—but that it appears at all shows the strength and persistence of this element in Crabbe's temper.

The civil dudgeon is ended by a storm which the poet describes with characteristically scrupulous accuracy over both the appearance of the external world and its impact on himself:

> Now on the colder water faintly shone
> The sloping light—the cheerful day was gone;
> Frown'd every cloud, and from the gather'd frown
> The thunder burst, and rain came pattering down.

My torpid senses now my fears obey'd,
When the fierce lightning on the eye-balls play'd.
Now, all the freshness of the morning fled,
My spirits burden'd, and my heart was dead.[1]

Even when the storm is over, the calm that follows is not the serenity of the morning; it is not 'Pleasure revived, but Misery forgot'.

The abrupt end of his story brings the author back to a new awareness of the present, and the power of memory as an anodyne is over. He begins to think again of the rest of his life, which was prefigured, in little, in the boating excursion. Despite the diversity of incident, the same pattern has been repeated in the experience of many other days:

> All Promise they—all Joy as they began!
> But Joy grew less, and vanish'd as they ran!
> Errors and evils came in many a form,—
> The mind's delusion, and the passions' storm.

But if reminiscence can no longer console, it has served a purpose beyond that of an anodyne. The poet's mind is now sufficiently collected to admit the truth that the same pattern was repeated in his marriage also. He records this knowledge, finally, in a mood of resignation which has been self-imposed by the process we have witnessed:

> The promised joy, that like this morning rose,
> Broke on my view, then clouded at its close;

[1] It is not consistently the accuracy of the naturalist in the usual sense of the word. 'Colder water' and 'sloping light' reveal the naturalist; but the use of words like 'frown' and 'fierce' link the external world with the feelings of the child. Crabbe often conveys his sense of a certain correspondence between our impressions of external nature and the moods in which we observe nature, but he never implies that anything akin to human emotion is inherent in nature. It is not his faith that every flower enjoys the air it breathes.

E'en Love himself, that promiser of bliss,
Made his best days of pleasure end like this:
He mix'd his bitters in the cup of joy
Nor gave a bliss uninjured by alloy.

The alloy had been considerable: an engagement lasting some ten years because Crabbe was too poor to marry earlier, and the clouding of the last seventeen years of his married life through Mrs. Crabbe's being subject, after the loss of a son in 1796, to alternate periods of dejection and excessive elation. And yet 'the mind's delusion and the passions' storm' are two of the main preoccupations of Crabbe's poetry.

II

POETIC AIMS AND CRITICAL RESPONSES

I

THROUGHOUT his poetic career Crabbe's chief aim was to please both himself and his readers by presenting the truth. In *The Village* he set out to paint 'the real Picture of the Poor', substituting for the drowsy and nebulous charms of pastoral verse a description of the kind of village and villagers that anyone who took the trouble to go and look might find on the frowning East Anglian coast. He continued to keep his eye steadily fixed upon his object, and to concern himself with very much the same kind of object. *The Parish Register* was (to quote his own account) 'an endeavour once more to describe village manners, not by adopting the notion of pastoral simplicity, or assuming ideas of rustic barbarity, but by more natural views of the peasantry, considered as a mixed body of persons'. In *The Borough* and the *Tales* of 1812 he somewhat shifted his ground socially, and concentrated on 'that order of society . . . which is placed between the humble and the great'. And in *Tales of the Hall* the change in social emphasis becomes more marked; here most of the characters are 'of superior class, though not the most elevated; and, with a few exceptions, are of educated and cultivated minds and habits'.

Crabbe's main interest, however, was never in accurate description of the social *scene*, but in the truthful presentation of human nature. His passion for observation

45

and his delight in the analysis of character made the social rank of his subject a matter of psychological and artistic, rather than sociological, importance. The label 'poet of the poor', which still sticks to his name, is misleading. Not much of his work is devoted to describing abject poverty: the kind of human material which was most congenial to him as a literary artist and as an observer was not furnished by those who were barely on the subsistence level; he could not have written very much about them without repeating himself. When he writes in detail of the abjectly poor, he usually treats them as a group or class. If they are shown as individuals, we see them through the eyes of others and do not learn much about what is going on in their minds: in the later pages of *Resentment* (*Tales*, XVII) the old man is rather a 'poor, bare, forked animal' than anything else. Crabbe seems to have found that, although persons even very slightly above the level of subsistence have a certain margin of personality or personal feelings and ideas, which can be explored—as in *Ellen Orford* (*The Borough*, Letter XX)—those whose efforts are exhausted in simply continuing to subsist scarcely can be presented as individuals, since there is no scope for personal peculiarity. The advantage of the 'middling classes', in his view, was that in them 'more originality of character, more variety of fortune, will be met with; because, on the one hand, they do not live in the eye of the world, and, therefore, are not kept in awe by the dread of observation and indecorum; neither, on the other, are they debarred by their want of means from the cultivation of mind and the pursuits of wealth and ambition, which are necessary to the developement of character displayed in the variety of situations to which this class is liable'.[1] The social scene is roughly analogous to the habitat of a plant: the plant will grow better in some soils than in others, but in any soil it will be the same species of plant.

In the final Letter of *The Borough* there is a passage describing the pleasure the poet takes in studying and recording human nature:

> For this the Poet looks the world around,
> Where form and life and reasoning man are found:
> He loves the mind, in all its modes, to trace,
> And all the manners of the changing race;
> Silent he walks the road of life along,
> And views the aims of its tumultuous throng:
> He finds what shapes the Proteus-passions take,
> And what strange waste of life and joy they make,
> And loves to show them in their varied ways,
> With honest blame or with unflattering praise:
> 'Tis good to know, 'tis pleasant to impart,
> These turns and movements of the human heart;
> The stronger features of the soul to paint,
> And make distinct the latent and the faint;
> MAN AS HE IS, to place in all men's view.[2]

This reads like an uncompromising assertion of the worth of realistic poetry. In Crabbe's day it was necessary to defend this kind of poetry, and the poet makes his defence in the preface to the *Tales* of 1812, in which are to be found his most carefully considered statements on his art. He has, he says, described men, manners and things as faithfully as he could. He knows there are those who think that writing of this kind is not poetry,

[1] *Works*, III, p. 13. The passage is from one of Crabbe's note-books.
[2] *Ibid.* IV, p. 94; ll. 426-40.

but protests that it is unjust to applaud accuracy and fidelity of representation in portrait- or landscape-painting while denying the name of poetry to 'verses which strongly and faithfully delineate character and manners'. The name should not be reserved for 'lofty and heroic' compositions or for productions of the kind of poet who is 'of imagination all compact' and, 'in the excursions of his fancy between heaven and earth, lights upon a kind of fairy-land, in which he places a creation of his own, where he embodies shapes, and gives action and adventure to his ideal offspring'.[1]

Crabbe is willing to concede that this lofty type of poetry alone has pretensions to inspiration, but firmly asserts that authentic poetry may be produced, without the prompting of 'inspiration', by those who 'address their productions to the plain sense and sober judgment of their readers, rather than to their fancy and imagination'. Unless this is granted, he points out, 'a vast deal of what has been hitherto received as genuine poetry would no longer be entitled to that appellation'. He then gives an impressive list of the kinds of writing which would be excluded by the narrow definition of poetry he is combating; what he thought valuable in the sober order of poetry is clear from the terms in which the list is couched:

All that kind of satire wherein character is skilfully delineated ... many affecting narratives which are founded on real events, and borrow no aid whatever from the imagination of the writer, must likewise be rejected: a considerable part of the poems, as they have hitherto been denominated, of Chaucer, are of this naked and unveiled character: and there are in his Tales many pages of coarse, accurate, and minute, but very striking description.

[1] *Works*, IV, p. 142.

Many small poems in a subsequent age, of most impressive kind, are adapted and addressed to the common sense of the reader, and prevail by the strong language of truth and nature: they amused our ancestors, and they continue to engage our interest, and excite our feelings, by the same powerful appeals to the heart and affections. In times less remote, Dryden has given us much of this poetry, in which the force of expression and accuracy of description have neither needed nor obtained assistance from the fancy of the writer . . . Pope himself has no small portion of this actuality of relation, this nudity of description, and poetry without an atmosphere; the lines beginning 'In the worst inn's worst room,' are an example, and many others may be seen in his Satires, Imitations, and above all in his Dunciad.[1]

Crabbe, reopening Warton's notorious question, whether Pope was a poet, echoes Johnson's retort: 'To circumscribe poetry by a definition will only shew the narrowness of the definer, though a definition which shall exclude Pope will not easily be made', and tartly observes that 'an author will find comfort in his expulsion from the rank and society of Poets, by reflecting that men much his superiors were likewise shut out, and more especially when he finds also that men not much his superiors are entitled to admission'.

He does not seek to make a distinction between poetry of the head and of the heart. When he praises poems 'adapted to the common sense of the reader' which 'engage our interest, and excite our feelings, by . . . *powerful appeals to the heart and affections*', he is asserting that 'invented life' has, for the poet, no advantage over 'real life'. Poems describing actuality, he insists, achieve specifically poetic effects:

I must allow that the effect of poetry should be to lift the mind from the painful realities of actual existence, from its every-day

[1] *Ibid.* IV, pp. 143-4.

concerns, and its perpetually-occurring vexations, and to give it repose by substituting objects in their place which it may contemplate with some degree of interest and satisfaction: but, what is there in all this, which may not be effected by a fair representation of existing character?

And here he launches a counter-attack:

nay, by a faithful delineation of those painful realities, those every-day concerns, and those perpetually-occurring vexations themselves, provided they be not (which is hardly to be supposed) the very concerns and distresses of the reader? for when it is admitted that they have no particular relation to him, but are the troubles and anxieties of other men, they excite and interest his feelings as the imaginary exploits, adventures, and perils of romance;—they soothe his mind, and keep his curiosity pleasantly awake; they appear to have enough of reality to engage his sympathy, but possess not interest sufficient to create painful sensations.[1]

The poet's representations of life, then, must meet two requirements: they must have enough of reality to engage the reader's sympathy, but the material represented must have no particular relation to the reader—he must have no sense of being personally involved.

Crabbe continues his counter-attack by insisting that even fictions must temporarily have the effect of realities:

Fiction itself, we know, and every work of fancy, must for a time have the effect of realities; nay, the very enchanters, spirits, and monsters of Ariosto and Spenser must be present in the mind of the reader while he is engaged by their operations, or they would be as the objects and incidents of a nursery tale to a rational understanding, altogether despised and neglected.

The important thing is 'the manner in which the poem itself is conducted'; if that is 'judiciously managed' fact

[1] *Works*, pp. 146-7.

and fiction will make the same kind of impression on 'the concurring feelings of the reader' because both will appear to be taken from truth and nature.

The poet does not say explicitly what he means by 'judicious management', but his demand that the objects it presents must temporarily have the effect of realities and be present in the mind of the reader brings us back to the question of 'actuality of relation'. Crabbe never forgets that, strictly speaking, nature cannot be augmented (much less invented) by the poet, though it may be modified in the representation. He himself tries to delineate nature with only that modification demanded by his art, or by prudence and charity. To a friend who asked whether his men and women were 'really existing creatures' or beings imagined by the poet, he replied:

... there is not one of whom I had not in my mind the original; but I was obliged, in some cases, to take them from their real situations, in one or two instances to change even the sex, and, in many, the circumstances. The nearest to real life was the proud, ostentatious man in the 'Borough' [Sir Denys Brand, Letter XIII], who disguises an ordinary mind by doing great things; but the others approach to reality at greater or less distances. Indeed, I do not know that I could paint merely from my own fancy; and there is no cause why we should. Is there not diversity sufficient in society?[1]

It is his aim to clarify nature:

> The stronger features of the soul to paint,
> And make distinct the latent and the faint.

Only thus can the object described be made as if present in the reader's mind. The reader must be made to see more clearly in art than he does in nature, and the poet

[1] *Life*, p. 232; letter to Mary Leadbeater dated 1 December 1816.

must therefore discard the accidentals of his original and concentrate attention on what he considers significant. To Crabbe it is not only the stronger features that are significant; he endeavours to disclose the latent and the faint too, still preserving proportion between the strong and the faint. What he strives to avoid is presenting the object modified by any passion of his own; and it is largely his unparalleled care to strip his object of purely personal impressions and emotional hazes (except when the haze *is* the object) that enables him to present what is paradoxically—for all its fidelity to nature—peculiarly his own world.[1]

Crabbe appears to have underrated either his own 'actuality of relation' or his readers' susceptibilities; he thought they would find his poems less painful than they in fact did. Yet it is clear from his remarks on poetry about painful realities that he recognised a relation between the reader's enjoyment of poetry and the emotional distance separating him from the experience about which he reads. And he is consistent in maintaining that satisfaction can be derived from reading about painful subjects. The preface of 1812 is not his first statement on the matter; he had already set forth his views in an astringent passage referring to the Letter on prisons (*The Borough*, XXIII). Descriptions of misery, he says here, make no material impression on the mind; they have not the 'strength and solidity of

---

[1] He knew well enough that in actual life the appearance of objects varies according to the mood of the beholder. The purpose of *The Lover's Journey* (*Tales*, X) is to describe the successive changes in the lover's impressions of a landscape brought about by pleasurable anticipation, jealous gloom and absorption in the company of his mistress, these subjective landscapes being contrasted with accounts of the countryside as it 'really' was.

truth placed before our eyes'—and yet even real sufferings have no very serious or lasting effect on the minds of those who witness them.

But he hopes that his account of suffering and crime

will excite, in some minds, that mingled pity and abhorrence, which, *while it is not unpleasant to the feelings*, is useful in its operation. It ties and binds us to all mankind by sensations common to us all, and in some degree connects us, without degradation, even to the most miserable and guilty of our fellow-men.[1]

Evidently he believed that the value of work like the Letters on poorhouses and prisons lay partly in their salutary moral effect. Nevertheless, except in his earlier work, *direct* moral or social instruction seldom forms a major part of Crabbe's purpose. It is true, the power of making moral and social judgments has affected, at some stage in the processes of observation and composition, almost everything he wrote. As so much of his material consists of studies of conduct it would be odd if this were not so, given his habits of mind. But this does not make him a didactic poet, in intention or in effect. He investigates the facts of conduct, including its motives, and imparts the results of his investigation. He also judges conduct, and his judgments are present in the finished poems, often implicitly rather than explicitly. But the presentation of fact is not distorted by the judgment.

Crabbe more than once disclaims the intention of instructing his readers—he regarded his poems, after all, as the fruits of his leisure. But if he does not strive to improve, he takes care not to injure. His vigilance in this matter appears to come from an awareness that the

[1] *Works*, IV, p. 57. My italics.

'yielding minds of the young' are easily confused and misled, and that most readers lack the necessary capacity for a discriminating analysis of character. The explanatory notes which accompany *Abel Keene* and *Peter Grimes* (*The Borough*, XXI, XXII) and *Arabella* (*Tales*, IX) show the author's anxiety lest the hasty or unperceptive reader has not noticed all he should have done; but the shortcomings will have been the reader's, not the poet's. It is significant that Crabbe prefers to write notes rather than mar his tales with too many moral or psychological 'signposts'.

He does not regret the limitation of the poet's scope for reasons of practical morality. Some material, on the other hand, he rejects as artistically intractable—he speaks in the preface to *The Borough* of 'the utter repugnancy which subsists between the studies and objects of topography and poetry'. But when no such considerations are involved, he is not prepared to make undue concessions to the tastes of his readers (especially the more squeamish), for he sees that a writer who is afraid of giving offence to a single reader is likely to produce merely insipid work. He confines himself to subjects he feels able to handle competently. The 'great subjects of religion' and patriotic themes he had attempted, with results which dissatisfied him. But he knew, for all his bland deference towards his critics, what subjects did lie within his range, and he knew that this range included themes which many poets would be prudent to shun. The tone in which he refers to a poem which might expose him to a charge of presumption in the choice of subject is modest but certainly not diffident:

In the story of 'Sir Eustace Grey,' an attempt is made to describe the wanderings of a mind first irritated by the consequences of

error and misfortune, and afterwards soothed by a species of en-
thusiastic conversion, still keeping him insane; a task very difficult; and, if the presumption of the attempt may find pardon, it
will not be refused to the failure of the poet. It is said of our
Shakespeare, respecting madness,—

'In that circle none dare walk but he:'—

yet be it granted to one, who dares not to pass the boundary fixed
for common minds, at least to step near to the tremendous verge,
and form some idea of the terrors that are stalking in the inter-
dicted space.[1]

'With me the way I take is not a matter of choice,
but of necessity.' Crabbe is speaking, here, of the
arrangement of material in his *Tales*; but he might have
said this truthfully enough about his poetry in general.
He seldom attempted what he was not sure he could
perform. Conversely, as his critics have on the whole
agreed, he could perform what he attempted. It is on
the value and acceptability of the performance that
opinions have differed.

II

We have seen what Crabbe thought about his own
poetry: it is also relevant to consider what some of his
contemporaries thought. They have the advantage of us
in one important respect—they are more acutely aware
than ourselves of the relation of his work to the poetic
principles and practice of the century in which he was
born.

Anyone brought up in eighteenth-century ways of
thought about poetry would be able to make something
of Crabbe. Even a perfunctory reading of his work

[1] Preface to 1807 *Poems*; *Works*, II, pp. 21-2.

shows him to be conspicuously of the old school in some respects: he commands the descriptive, didactic and satirical modes of writing; he strives after 'truth to Nature'; his diction, for all its unevenness, is not often wholly incongruous with eighteenth-century practice in one or another of the poetic 'kinds', and, indeed, conforms fairly punctiliously with the canons of the age in the earlier work; he prefers a staple eighteenth-century metre, the heroic couplet, and, with very few exceptions, works most easily when he adopts this metre. He is professedly a follower of Dryden and Pope and does not claim to be doing anything strikingly new.

Yet from the first Crabbe was seen to be not only an upholder of the eighteenth-century poetic tradition, but also an original poet. Johnson read *The Village* 'with great delight' and found it 'original, vigorous, and elegant'.[1] Jeffrey, who commends Crabbe as a supporter of the old school, also describes him, with steadily increasing warmth, as 'one of the most original, nervous, and pathetic poets of the present century', 'the most original writer who has ever come before us', and the writer of 'some of the most original and powerful poetry that the world has ever seen'.[2] Even so hostile a critic as Hazlitt credits him with a power of original portraiture.

Jeffrey finds little or no difficulty in reconciling Crabbe's traditionalism with his originality. He points to affinities of style with Dryden, Pope, Johnson and Goldsmith, and observes that 'there are so few of his contemporaries to whom Mr. Crabbe bears any resemblance, that we can scarcely explain our opinion of

[1] Letter to Reynolds, quoted by Crabbe's son, *Life*, pp. 118-19.
[2] *Essays from 'The Edinburgh Review'*, ed. cit. pp. 287, 359, 361.

his merits, without comparing him to some of his predecessors'.[1] This was a point in the poet's favour, and Jeffrey concludes his review by expressing the hope that Crabbe 'will soon appear again among the worthy supporters of the old poetical establishment, and come in time to surpass the revolutionists in fast firing, as well as in weight of metal'.[2] But the critic is, quite properly, more often concerned with defining the poet's originality. He notes his force and truth of description, finds him distinguished from other poets in choosing to write of ordinary characters taken from the lower ranks of life, and truly observes of the poet of *The Borough* that 'not only has he nothing prodigious or astonishing in any of his representations, but he has not even attempted to impart any of the ordinary colours of poetry to these vulgar materials'.[3] It is original, says Jeffrey, to be the satirist of low life, yet the poet's originality is more valuably shown in the unvarnished veracity of his work, in his 'lively, touching, and finely contrasted representations of the dispositions, sufferings, and occupations' of the ordinary majority. Reviewing the *Tales*, he praises Crabbe for exploring ground ignored by other poets through social prejudice:

. . . he has traced out the course of those rich and lovely veins in the rude and unpolished masses that lie at the bottom of society; and unfolded, in the middling orders of the people, the workings of those finer feelings, and the stirrings of those loftier emotions which the partiality of other poets had attributed, almost exclusively, to actors on a higher scene.[4]

The warmest and most varied eulogy is to be found in the review of *Tales of the Hall*. The poet is credited with

[1] *Ibid.* p. 288 (review of the *Poems* of 1807). [2] *Ibid.* p. 306.
[3] *Ibid.* p. 307. [4] *Ibid.* pp. 335-6.

. . . an unrivalled and almost magical power of observation, resulting in descriptions so true to nature as to strike us rather as transcripts than imitations, an anatomy of character and feeling not less exquisite and searching, an occasional touch of matchless tenderness, and a deep and dreadful pathetic, interspersed by fits, and strangely interwoven with the most minute and humble of his details. Add to all this the sure and profound sagacity with which he every now and then startles us in the midst of very unambitious discussion; and the weight and terseness of the maxims which he drops, like oracular responses, on occasions that give no promise of such a revelation; and last, though not least, that sweet and seldom sounded chord of Lyrical inspiration, the lightest touch of which instantly charms away all harshness from his numbers, all lowness from his themes, and at once exalts him to a level with the most energetic and inventive poets of his age.[1]

These are the views of a man of conservative but not inflexible taste. Jeffrey responded readily to the traditional in Crabbe, but was able to adjust himself to what was new or not in keeping with eighteenth-century notions—he could see in what way the older mode was being reshaped, and how a certain reshaping was demanded by the poet's purposes. He does not, however, explicitly state the principal reason why this disciple of the old school came to direct the current of his poetry along what proved at length a quite distinct and little-explored channel. Crabbe singles out *one* element common to the work of Dryden and Pope—and of Chaucer before them—which he finds himself able to develop: actuality of relation. But because he concentrates on a single element in three dissimilar and versatile poets, the result of his labours is not simply imitation but exploration. Jeffrey's mining metaphor is suggestive:

[1] *Op. cit.* pp. 361-2.

Crabbe discovers rich veins of ore not previously brought to light.

It is usual to allow Crabbe the merit of being 'true to nature'. But the phrase is vague, and needs elucidation. Jeffrey is again helpful:

Mr. Crabbe . . . shows us something which we have all seen, or may see, in real life; and draws from it such feelings and such reflections as every human being must acknowledge that it is calculated to excite. He delights us by the truth, and vivid and picturesque beauty of his representations, and by the force and pathos of the sensations with which we feel they are connected.[1]

The poet's representations of character and sentiment are 'drawn from that eternal and universal standard of truth and nature, which everyone is knowing enough to recognise, and no one great enough to depart from with impunity'. They have nothing of the capricious or idiosyncratic. The poet not only describes what is to be seen in real life, but also refrains from trying to capture our attention by telling us what he personally feels about it. He is not exclusively concerned with the typical (nor does Jeffrey demand this), but he fastens on what is central in each character, not on the peripheral or accidental. He shows general human characteristics together with those peculiar to the persons he describes.

This was what 'truth to nature' meant to Jeffrey and many of his readers in the earliest years of the nineteenth century. It came to mean something rather different, to Crabbe; but Jeffrey's comments apply well enough to most of what he had written when Jeffrey's review of the 1807 *Poems* appeared. In *The Village* we have a representative old labourer suffering a representative fate; the minor figures, too—the self-important,

---

[1] *Ibid*. p. 289 (Review of *Poems* of 1807).

incompetent physician and the 'murmuring nurse'—
are sufficiently typical. The only feature in Crabbe's
account of village life which cannot be called typical
is the behaviour of the clergyman who ('detained
by weightier care'—viz., sport) does not attend the
pauper's funeral to read the burial service; and the poet
is careful to supply a footnote explaining that this kind
of behaviour, though uncommon, is not unknown.

But a change may already be discerned in *The Parish
Register*. 'Characters' form the staple of this work.
Crabbe shows us many significant varieties of villager,
usually bringing out clearly the ruling passion in which
the character's relation to the 'universal standard of
truth and nature' appears most conspicuously, and the
chief social and economic factors which determine the
mode in which the ruling passion operates. But he
knows perfectly well that human nature has a com-
plexity to which delineation in terms of ruling passions
cannot do justice, and he already seems to be growing
more interested in portraying the individual: hence the
sketches of Richard Monday, the charity-boy who becomes rich, of the surly but sensible Roger Cuff, and of
Dibble the sexton. The concern with the individual is
carried even further in *The Borough*. Typical scenes,
characters and occupations still appear, and the links
between the general or universal and the particular or
local are made clear; but this is done partly to indicate
the background against which, in the later parts of the
poem, we are to see a succession of individuals. It is in
connection with *The Borough* that Crabbe emphasises
the advantage of the middle class as literary material—
they afford originality of character and variety of fortune.

Although, then, truth to nature is his constant aim,

his emphasis shifts away from the solely representative. As often as not, especially in the later work, this concern for truth shows itself in the tracing of some common human characteristic in unlikely circumstances in which its presence might have been unsuspected or overlooked. And Crabbe likes to show universal or 'master' passions in rudimentary form, or in disguise, or so closely interwoven with other matter that they can only be detected by an unusually vigilant eye.

If he begins by showing us something we have all seen or may see, he ends by showing us what we may see only if we look closely enough. As for the appropriateness of feeling and reflection to be found in the tales, they can scarcely be appreciated by every human being (as Jeffrey believed to be true of the earlier work), but only by those who read with that peculiar kind of co-operation with the poet which Crabbe's work demands. The ground of the sympathy aroused still lies in the situations presented in the poem and not in any analysis of the poet's own feeling about them, and it is still an intelligible ground of sympathy; but it is not obvious. Confronting a multitude of details, of which some would be noticed by any observer and some overlooked, Crabbe is far from discarding the kind which would be overlooked. This is partly because he was convinced that much of what was overlooked ought to be scrutinised, both on moral grounds and because (if 'judiciously managed') it was a source of satisfaction poetically. It is partly, too, because of his delight in exercising his powers of observation, irrespectively of the poetry in which his findings might ultimately be embodied. But beyond this is his firm belief that truth —and more particularly truth about human nature—

can be attained by scrutiny and is well worth attaining. Jeffrey speaks of him as 'fitting in his little window in [the] breasts [of his subjects], and applying his tests and instruments of observation', and setting himself about 'a minute and curious scrutiny of their whole habits, history, adventures, and dispositions'.[1] The poet himself, apostrophising 'fair Truth', asks her help in seeing people as they really are:

> . . . let me clearly see
> The minds I paint, as they are seen in thee; . . .
> And closely let me view the naked human heart.[2]

Many people, while granting that Crabbe is true to nature, have complained that he viewed things much too closely, and recorded too much of what he saw. Yet it was largely this minute accuracy that held the attention of his contemporaries. Hazlitt remarks that he 'relies for the effect of novelty on the microscopic minuteness with which he dissects the most trivial objects', and observes of the lines in *The Borough* describing the dull scenes over which the morose Peter Grimes brooded:

This is an exact *fac-simile* of some of the most unlovely parts of the creation. Indeed, the whole of Mr. Crabbe's *Borough* . . . is done so to the life, that it seems almost like some sea-monster, crawled out of the neighbouring slime, and harbouring a breed of strange vermin, with a strong local scent of tar and bulge-water.[3]

It seemed to Hazlitt that Crabbe's career had begun at a time when the public was disposed to welcome painter-like poets:

---

[1] *Op. cit.* p. 370.
[2] *Tales of the Hall*, I; *Works*, VI, p. 23; ll. 121-5.
[3] *The Spirit of the Age, ed. cit.*, pp. 243, 248.

a taste for that sort of poetry, which leans for support on the truth and fidelity of its imitations of nature began to display itself much about that time [*i.e.* the time of the composition of *The Village*], and, in a good measure, in consequence of the direction of the public taste to the subject of painting.[1]

The 'eye for nature', enfeebled and perverted by book-learning, 'the accumulation of wordy commonplaces, the gaudy pretensions of poetical fiction', would tend, Hazlitt argues, to be restored by a study of the fine arts. This factor no doubt helped to make Crabbe's poetry popular; but his own eye for nature was trained by the study of botany and entomology far more than by such study of painting as he made.

Yet even if we attribute his popularity to the fashionable study of the fine arts, we have still to ask why the public should delight in facsimiles (whether done on canvas or in words) of 'the most unlovely parts of the creation'. It is partly, Jeffrey assures us (in conformity with current theory), that 'the perception of a perfect and successful imitation' pleases—he thinks that much of the pleasure to be derived from reading Crabbe's poetry may be referred to its 'mere truth and fidelity'. Hazlitt has another reason to suggest:

Mr. Crabbe is one of the most popular and admired of our living authors. That he is so, can be accounted for on no other principle than the strong ties that bind us to the world about us and our involuntary yearnings after whatever in any manner powerfully and directly reminds us of it.[2]

The critic is not thinking of 'universal nature' and the 'primary affections', but of trivial, local and particular details of 'what happens in every place of the kingdom

[1] *Ibid.* p. 245.   [2] *Ibid.* p. 243.

every hour of the year'. It is not that familiar things are made new, but that we are powerfully reminded of their existence.

Jeffrey, unlike Hazlitt, saw very well that Crabbe was not merely a literal imitator of things that his readers had already observed; he was one who made them see clearly what lay before their eyes without their noticing it. His immediate purpose was to give them a distinct view of the commonplace, and not only the *visible* commonplace:

The poet of humble life *must* describe a good deal, and must even describe, minutely, many things which possess in themselves no beauty or grandeur.[1]

Jeffrey wants his readers to get rid of lingering eighteenth-century prejudice against minute particulars *as* particulars; and he lays down new regulations concerning the degree of minuteness to be allowed in the representation of humble life. Minute detail fulfils a necessary, though ancillary, function. The poet has to describe externals minutely in order to give 'locality and imaginary reality' to his characters, and to make their common condition clear. Against such a background 'peculiar and selected groups' can be presented with advantage. Characters, as well as externals, must be studied with minute and anatomical precision, for the readers must see the 'ordinary traits and general family features of the beings among whom they are to move, before they can either understand, or take much interest in the individuals who are to engross their attention'. All these things help forward the interest or the 'pathos' of the picture.

[1] *Op. cit.* p. 313.

64

Jeffrey credits Crabbe with a purpose beyond that of accurate description, and, correspondingly, with producing other effects in the reader besides the pleasure of perceiving a perfect imitation. He introduces into his argument issues which are social or moral and not aesthetic; this is especially striking when he is dealing with poetry on themes from common life—'low' subjects. Jeffrey can hardly be blamed for the confusion which existed about this matter, but he did little to dispel it. He observed, justly enough, that the prevalent dislike of 'low' subjects in poetry was grounded largely in social prejudice, and that works of art treating low subjects were not, therefore, necessarily low works of art. But his approval of poetry on themes from humble life has a moral basis. He expects readers to respond to characters in poetry very much as they might respond to actual persons; but he would like them to read as enlightened and benevolent citizens, and he believes that, by a fairly simple process, a reading of Crabbe's best work will increase their enlightenment and benevolence. Poetry, he says, stimulates the imagination, heart and fancy into activity; it fosters in the reader feelings which are morally and socially valuable. In the course of our everyday experience there accumulate in our hearts 'an infinite multitude of little fragments of sympathy with our brethren in humble life, abortive movements of compassion, and embryos of kindness and concern'. But because of the 'selfish bustle and fever of our daily occupations' they have withered. These fragments and embryos, Jeffrey believes, the poet is able to revive and carry on to maturity.[1]

He has no complaint to make if the poet writes on

[1] *Ibid.* p. 311.

painful themes (more especially since he finds in Crabbe 'great mastery over the tragic passions of pity and horror'). But he firmly excludes part of humanity from the sphere of literature, as 'disgusting'. His criterion here is a moral one. 'Disgusting' characters (all too frequent, he complains, in Crabbe) are 'the depraved, abject, diseased, and neglected poor—creatures in whom everything amiable or respectable has been extinguished by sordid passions or brutal debauchery; who have no means of doing the mischief of which they are capable, whom everyone despises, and no one can either love or fear'. When we meet such persons, either in literature or in life, says Jeffrey, they cannot arouse pity or horror, but only disgust; as readers of poetry 'we feel our imaginations polluted by the intrusion of any images connected with them'.

But such statements do no more than contradict what Crabbe had said in *The Borough* of descriptions of suffering and crime—that they excite 'that mingled pity and abhorrence, which, while it is not unpleasant to the feelings, . . . binds us to all mankind by sensations common to us all, and in some degree connects us, without degradation, even to the most miserable and guilty of our fellow-men'. In his view, a reminder to the reader that he belonged to the same species as these depraved and abject people could not possibly be degrading: they were, in fact, fellow-men.

However, Jeffrey had less occasion to harp on this string when he reviewed Crabbe's later tales. In the *Tales* of 1812 he already discerned a more amiable and consoling view of human nature; but it was *Tales of the Hall* that brought home to him fully the comprehensiveness and subtlety of the poet's portrayal of human nature and made him recognise that Crabbe's chief interest lay in investigating and revealing human nature and not in conveying moral or social lessons. Still, he is able to add a little about the moral effect which this will have on the reader. The fruits of prolonged and discriminating observation, unlike those of satire, will not so much cast down the proud as raise the lowly; we shall learn to judge human nature truly—our promptitude to admire or envy will be corrected, our curiosity stimulated, our tolerance increased, and our sympathies extended and better directed.

Crabbe would certainly have been gratified to find that his poems did indeed produce these happy results, but there are no signs that he confidently hoped they would do so. He did not believe that habits of thinking and feeling were readily changed by literature. He was wiser than his critic in claiming that if his work merited attention it did so as poetry and not as social or moral propaganda.

It is noteworthy that Jeffrey, as well as Hazlitt, found that Crabbe impressed the reader somewhat against his will. He is too much the anatomist, Jeffrey sighs, and some of his laboriously exhibited specimens are dull, though 'he succeeds more frequently than could have been anticipated.' Hazlitt words it more bluntly: 'He rivets attention by being tedious.' Yet neither critic explains exactly how this compulsion is exerted.

To treat unpromising material, to admit (to insist, even) that 'Man as he is' is apparently commonplace, and yet to achieve a portrayal that rivets attention: this demands a considerable and peculiar power. Crabbe's belief that the effect of poetry arises from the poet's power to make realities as if present in the reader's mind gives us the most useful clue towards an understanding of this peculiar power. We have three questions to consider: What constitutes actuality of relation? How are moral values involved? (For although Crabbe is not a didactic poet, he is firmly convinced that moral values are realities.) And in what does the judicious management of a poem lie?

'POETRY WITHOUT AN ATMOSPHERE'

I

I F a writer is to record faithfully, in 'poetry without an atmosphere', material drawn from the actual world, he must strive after the greatest possible transparency of treatment. The character of the material he uses will do much to determine the prevailing tone of the poem. The less the reader's awareness of the medium through which the reality is conveyed and the greater his awareness of the reality itself, the better will the poet have succeeded. And yet complete transparency is impossible. The poet cannot be simply a neutral transmitter or verbaliser; however long and deliberate his scrutiny, however great his care to present the actual, he cannot give a wholly impersonal picture.

The poetry of Crabbe has certainly great actuality. What 'atmosphere' it has is 'dry light'; all the objects stand out very distinctly. We are made to feel that the eye of common sense has observed the scene, but that it has looked longer and more closely than it does for everyday purposes. Nevertheless, what the poet gives us is a selective arrangement of the various impressions made on him by people and scenes he has observed or heard about. Moreover, although it is possible to find passages in which he appears to aim at doing no more than make an image of actuality, in his work as a whole criticism accompanies description or narration. This critical spirit is shown in various ways. Sometimes it is overt, and appears as the straightforward statement of 'moral truths' in the form of sententious passages or brief sagacious comments. Sometimes, when the satirist is at work, it operates obliquely, but is still quite conspicuous. But in tales having a strong emotional tone, especially a tragic tone, both the direct moral comment and the satirical mode of criticism may be dispensed with at the crisis of the tale; for criticism can take the form of a tacit appeal (none the less powerful for being tacit) to moral standards which command general assent.[1] The reader is expected to make his own application of these standards to the particular set of characters and circumstances presented by the poet. In Crabbe, therefore, criticism may sometimes be said to consist in an eloquent silence.

II

This 'poetry without an atmosphere' is both homogeneous and varied. Its homogeneity does not come solely from the poet's restricting his material to the more or less commonplace. It comes also from the habits of thinking, feeling and expression which he brings to this material—from his unusually systematic

---

[1] Where the conduct represented does not require a grave response, it may escape explicit comment and yet be silently 'placed'. In *The Widow* (*Tales of the Hall*, XVII) the widow's rejection of a proposal of marriage is shown to be merely a tactical move by the abruptness of the poet's transition to the statement that the marriage takes place:

'Adieu! then, sir,' she added; 'thus you find
The changeless purpose of a steady mind,
In one now left alone, but to her fate resign'd.'

The marriage follow'd . . .

(*Works*, VII, p. 177).

scrutiny; from that keen and sensitive responsiveness to conduct which precedes and co-operates with judgment; from the unfailing assurance with which human beings are judged in accordance with a fairly simple and extremely stable moral code; and from a peculiar mode of expression which will be one of the chief themes of the present chapter. Crabbe's variety—which is much greater than is often assumed—has two main sources: a power of making fine distinctions in surveying material drawn from a socially restricted range; and an ability, while working as a rule within one broad poetic mode, to achieve precisely that tone which is most consonant with the object as the poet sees it and wants us to see it.

The poet's union of homogeneity with variety of tone cannot be best shown by the stylistic analysis of isolated passages. Certain exceptions, it is true, may be made. In some poems, especially the earlier ones (*The Village*, *Sir Eustace Grey*, *The Hall of Justice*), the prevailing tones are conspicuous, easy to classify, and capable of being illustrated by the quotation of verbal detail. And it is also easy, though not helpful, to describe the tone imparted to a passage by the deliberate assumption of a certain manner for writing that particular passage, as in the Letter on inns (*The Borough*, XI), in which the author facetiously employs an ornate style because of the prosaic nature of his topic. But this is an intentional affectation, and throws no more light on what is central in the tone of Crabbe's poetry than would an account of those jingles, puns and pretended antitheses with which his work is strewn, mannerisms which jar momentarily on the reader without affecting in an important way the passages in which they occur.

With the bulk of Crabbe's work, discrimination is far more difficult than with *The Village* or *Sir Eustace Grey*. This is because of his habitual and studied rejection of what Jeffrey calls 'the ordinary colours of poetry'. What *is* central, indeed, is the neutral or transparent manner in which matters of fact are conveyed. As we saw earlier, the poet defended his use of a naked and spare manner for poetry in which the aim was to make the object as if present in the reader's mind. He normally writes in a selection of the language really used by men (educated men, not rustics) in conversation or in letter-writing. This is not to say that a genuinely colloquial tone is much in evidence in Crabbe, or that he *combines* words in poetry as he would if he were writing prose.[1] But all that need be said here about his vocabulary is that, like his themes, it is taken from the everyday world. It is the kind of language which common sense would choose as the most immediately appropriate to its purpose.

If the words are uncoloured, the world which the poet uses them to convey is a world of 'incessant matters of fact'. In nearly every one of his works there is a large element of the informative and expository. Sometimes the professed purpose of the poem allows or demands this—ostensibly, at least, the purpose of *The Borough* or *The Parish Register* is to give the reader the information he needs if he is to form a distinct and accurate impression of a small seaport or a village. It is obvious that descriptive poetry offers the writer vast scope for presenting matters of fact. But it has its dangers for one who can do nothing but describe: he is likely to produce a tedious work that is without signifi-

[1] This subject is discussed below, Chapter VI.

cance as a whole. There seems to be no reason for quarrelling with the view that purely descriptive poetry is poetry of a low order. It would be idle to claim that Crabbe has always escaped the pitfalls of descriptive writing; yet much in his work that purports to be descriptive writing does something more than present facts, and is valuable for that reason. The tales, correspondingly, are more than bare recitals of events.

What we have to do is to discover how Crabbe makes a significant image of actuality by arranging and co-ordinating facts which have no significance if they are considered separately. Matter-of-factness is essential in narratives of the peculiar quality that we find in Crabbe. He habitually gives us little incident, together with copious data relating to the social position of the characters, and to their temperaments, habits and personal situation. The chain of events and the evolution of character revealed therein are only intelligible if these data have been fully assimilated. Among the data we find an abundance of material things: these are simplest kind of 'hard facts' in which Crabbe deals. There is much naming of articles of furniture, dress, ornaments and buildings, as well as objects taken from the sphere of inanimate nature. These are made to illustrate or reflect or symbolise aspects of human nature. The clothes worn by the characters, and the various objects with which they are surrounded, are presented in such a way that their relevance to the human being in the midst is clear. Dress may throw light on character or outlook; Abel Keene's change of fashion corresponds to his changed outlook (*The Borough*, XXI). The appearance of a room may reinforce our knowledge of its occupants; the untidy room in *The Elder Brother* (*Tales of the Hall*,

VII) suits the slatternly Rosabella, and the precise, tidy drawing-room described in *The Frank Courtship* (*Tales*, VI) is no less appropriate to its Quakerish owner. Or a room may be the visible counterpart of misery; this is true of the workhouse in which the disappointed painter dies (*Tales of the Hall*, III) and the garret in which the revengeful husband at length discovers his wife and her lover in *Sir Owen Dale* (*Tales of the Hall*, XII). There is very often a correspondence between external nature and a human mood. Occasionally Crabbe calls our attention to the connection, as in the story *Delay has Danger* (*Tales of the Hall*, XIII), where a passage describing the cheerless autumnal scene on which the despondent hero gazes is rounded off with the words:

> All these were sad in nature, or they took
> Sadness from him, the likeness of his look,
> And of his mind.

Peter Grimes (*The Borough*, XXII) chooses to hide from mankind amid scenery which reflects and intensifies his mood—mudbanks, with a 'lazy tide' creeping along the 'hot slimy channel'. *The Lover's Journey* (*Tales*, X) has as its theme the connection between the observer's mood and his impression of the scene before him; the tale illustrates the dictum with which the poem opens:

> It is the Soul that sees; the outward eyes
> Present the object, but the Mind descries;
> And thence delight, disgust, or cool indiff'rence rise.

Besides this, material objects are often to be regarded as tools used by the characters to perform good or evil or wise or foolish actions; and they may at the same time be symbols. The Widow Goe, nearing her end,

> dropp'd upon her knees,
> Heaven in her eye and in her hand her keys;
> And still the more she found her life decay,
> With greater force she grasp'd those signs of sway.

When at length she died, her sons (after shedding 'the tributary tear')

> from th' adhering clasp the keys unbound,
> And consolation for their sorrows found.[1]

Crabbe has explained the symbolic value of the keys ('those signs of sway'); but it is clear that they are not only symbols but also instruments having a practical use in ordinary life—they unlock doors and coffers, thus enabling the heirs to get at their money. Crabbe's more usual method is to show articles of this kind as instruments or tools, leaving us to deduce any symbolic significance they may have. In the tale of the Parish Clerk (of which more will be said later), the collection-plate, the coins, and the bran the Clerk puts into his pocket to prevent the coins from clinking as they are dropped in are the material tools with which the crime that ruins him is committed.

A different kind of co-ordination has to be noticed if we wish to discover how, with colourless words and intrinsically meaningless facts, Crabbe is able to impart to his poetry distinct and diverse tones. It will often be found that the characteristic tone of a poem or passage depends directly on the way in which the author has grouped his 'objects'. And it is only by seeing how a succession of groups is disposed that we can grasp his method of grading and contrasting the various tones which strike us in the poem as a whole. Crabbe's tales

[1] *The Parish Register*, III (*Burials*); *Works*, II, p. 207.

generally begin in a cool, neutral tone, which is used either for the concise recording of relevant facts, or for the statement of a social, moral or psychological generalisation which the tale is to illustrate. It is not possible, from the opening lines, to forecast whether the tale will be predominantly painful, pathetic, jocose or ironical. The 'temperature' may not rise far above the tepid throughout the tale, though more often than not there is considerable variation.

While the poem as a whole owes its complex tone to the grouping of variously-toned parts, the tone of any one of these smaller units (such as a brief description) may be determined to a great extent by its context. A passage which, taken in isolation, is a piece of purely factual description, often needs to be read with the context clearly in mind if we are to perceive its significance. It is itself illumined by what has gone before, and, in its turn, influences our response to what is to come. This may be illustrated by the description of the deserted mansion in *The Parish Register*:

> Next died the LADY who yon Hall possess'd;
> And here they brought her noble bones to rest.
> In Town she dwelt;—forsaken stood the Hall:
> Worms ate the floors, the tap'stry fled the wall:
> No fire the kitchen's cheerless grate display'd;
> No cheerful light the long-clos'd sash convey'd:
> The crawling worm, that turns a summer-fly,
> Here spun his shroud and laid him up to die
> The winter-death:—upon the bed of state,
> The bat shrill shrieking woo'd his flickering mate;
> To empty rooms the curious came no more,
> From empty cellars turn'd the angry poor,
> And surly beggars cursed the ever-bolted door.[1]

[1] *Works*, II, pp. 208-9; *Burials*, ll. 233-45.

Hitherto in *The Parish Register*, for all his insistence on the material surroundings of his villagers, Crabbe has been showing us a human society. But the lady of the manor, an absentee landlord, has not been a character in village life at all: her empty house is all that has been seen of her, and this house has, so to speak, pre-deceased its owner. The poet first arrests our attention by describing a building instead of a person, and then arouses our misgivings by conveying it in terms of decay, darkness and emptiness. The only life-cycle to be observed in the decaying house is that of worms and bats. It is not until the end of the passage that we hear of human beings there, of the anger of the poor and the curses of surly beggars. But we have been prepared by the factual description of the Hall for the criticism of the Lady which the poet wishes to make. We are encouraged to suspect that the poor are justly angry, since they have been deprived of what would have been given them as their due in a well-ordered Hall. There follows a sketch of the steward, 'the feeling servant' whose mediation between landlord and tenants has consisted in sparing the former all knowledge of the latter's complaints. This the 'feeble dame' was perfectly willing for him to do:

> She came not down, her falling groves to view;
> Why should she know, what one so faithful knew?
> Why come, from many clamorous tongues to hear,
> What one so just might whisper in her ear?
> Her oaks or acres, why with care explore;
> Why learn the wants, the sufferings of the poor;
> When one so knowing all their worth could trace,
> And one so piteous govern'd in her place?[1]

[1] *Ibid.* p. 209; ll. 252-9.

Crabbe has by now moved from factual description to caustic, if subdued, satire. But the ironical defence of the 'just' steward and the 'noble' Lady gains a melancholy overtone because the description of the forsaken house (a gloomy image of social irresponsibility) is present in our minds as we read the concluding lines of the passage—and Crabbe takes care to remind us of it in the ambiguous phrase 'falling groves'. In his account of the Lady's funeral and the disdainful 'Village-father's' words about her, he passes to a note of open condemnation which is much less remarkable. Without being wholly redundant, it amounts to little more than an explicit statement of what was already implicit. (This type of sequence is fairly common in Crabbe; and its final stage of somewhat morose and laboured didacticism cannot be attributed wholly to the poetic custom of the eighteenth century.)

The close of *The Widow* (*Tales of the Hall*, XVII) also shows how context can affect tone. The relevant lines here are not those in which Crabbe sums up the moral of the tale, but the description (which immediately precedes them) of the widow in her cottage:

> The widow'd lady to her cot retired,
> And there she lives delighted and admired:
> Civil to all, compliant and polite,
> Disposed to think, 'whatever is, is right;'
> She wears the widow's weeds, she gives the widow's mite.
> At home awhile, she in the autumn finds
> The sea an object for reflecting minds,
> And change for tender spirits; there she reads,
> And weeps in comfort in her graceful weeds.[1]

[1] *Works*, VII, p. 180; ll. 521-9.

If we disregard the context we find in this passage a subdued and gracious harmony, only a single line of which invites us to judge what is presented in any other way than as a 'twilight-piece':

And weeps in comfort in her graceful weeds.

This discloses a purely conventional mourning which scarcely veils the vanity and the desire for elegant comfort which are central to the widow's character. But certain other phrases are fully intelligible only in the light of what has gone before:

She wears the widow's weeds, she gives the widow's mite—

she has, we recall, learnt this decent parsimony from the extravagance of her late husband. Again, the lines

> . . . she in the autumn finds
> The sea an object for reflecting minds,
> And change for tender spirits;

can only be recognised as a piece of delicate irony if we remember what has been shown earlier—that the widow has very little capacity for reflection and that she merely affects sensibility. The window by which she sits not only gives her a view of the sea; it also gives the casual passer-by a view of the lady's well-preserved charms. She is to be taken for a vain and foolish but still attractive woman who has learnt a modicum of practical sense through experience. Her shortcomings have been exposed earlier in the tale, but there is a sober serenity at the close. The critical spirit is not absent, but it is subdued into a discreet and faintly amused tolerance: Crabbe gives us now the graceful and fragile façade of the widow's life.

It is necessary to insist on the importance of the two matters which have been considered in the preceding pages: first, the fact that the material objects which appear in Crabbe's images of actuality contribute not only to the accuracy of the image but also to its emotional and moral comprehensiveness; second, the fact that, unless the individual passage is constantly seen in relation to the poem as a whole, it is impossible to discern either the tone of that passage or the gradation of tone effected in the complete poem. For many of Crabbe's readers the poet's judicious management of his material has perhaps been obscured by the remarkable precision with which minutiae are presented, and by the leisureliness of his pace (a leisureliness not incompatible with terseness of style). He has been valued for the isolated passage rather than for the articulated whole. Now, as we have seen, even the isolated passage is by no means a haphazard collocation of details. (We may recall Jeffrey's remark: 'The pattern of his arabesque is so large, that there is no getting a fair specimen of it without taking in a good space'.[1]) And what is true of the passage is also true of the complete tale; here the pattern may be intricate in its convolutions. There is no doubt that the poet's power of articulation is seen to the best advantage in his tales, where other factors besides homogeneity of treatment and the purposeful gradation of tone play their part.[2] These other factors do not operate in *The Parish Register* and *The Borough* considered as wholes; the structural looseness of these works makes it natural that we should think of them as *collections* of sketches and tales. Nevertheless, in both works the homogeneity of treatment

[1] *Op. cit.* p. 382.   [2] These factors are discussed in the next chapter.

has a unifying tendency; and besides this (as the description of the deserted Hall shows) our response to the individual sketch is influenced by its relation to earlier sketches. This may be called articulation by means of ambience.

III

The consonance of tone for which Crabbe strives embraces moral decorum as well as strictly poetic decorum. The association between the two kinds of decorum is consistently maintained, and may be regarded as a distinct aspect of the poet's homogeneity. It would be difficult to say how far it is deliberate and how far a matter of habit. Sometimes it is certainly deliberate, and Crabbe refers to the subject quite explicitly, as in the tale of the Parish Clerk (*The Borough*, XIX). When he has proceeded some way in his story, he prepares us rather abruptly for a transition to a different tone, for he is coming to the serious part of the Clerk's history, and we must approach it in a suitable frame of mind:

> Thus far the playful Muse has lent her aid,
> But now departs, of graver theme afraid;
> Her may we seek in more appropriate time,—
> There is no jesting with distress and crime.

The jesting manner is absent, therefore, from the remainder of the tale. And yet this emphatic dismissal of the playful Muse scarcely seems to provide an adequate explanation of differences of tone between the beginning and end of the poem. Indeed, a close examination of the tale shows that whatever has been *deliberately* brought about through deference to decorum affects the tone of the author's interjections without radically affecting that of the main flow. Crabbe's practice was subtler than the above quotation would lead us to suppose.

The Parish Clerk is not one of his best tales, though it represents fairly what he could do in narrative at this stage of his career. But it seems worth detailed study for the light it throws on the question of poetic and moral decorum, and for the additional evidence it supplies of some of the features of Crabbe's work which have been considered earlier in the chapter.

Almost without exception, the tone of narration is carefully non-committal throughout the poem. To begin with, a character and a situation are presented. The central character, Jachin, is made the mouthpiece for his own point of view. The first discernible step which the poet takes to 'place' him is that of recording the Clerk's account of himself fully enough for its excessive zeal and assurance to stand out plainly. This not only provides us with a basis for judging Jachin's character, but also implants in our minds doubt about the genuineness and durability of his virtue; and this doubt is a necessary means of engaging our interest in the events that are to follow. Jachin is being given rope enough to hang himself: we wait to see first whether, and then how, he will do so. But the author has not yet intervened with his own interpretation. The Clerk's expression of his views constitutes a self-portrait of spiritual arrogance; he believes that his life is a series of victories over the devil, with whom he engages in single combat. Crabbe is confident that his reader's good sense will recognise that this attitude deserves reprobation. But it is a foolish as well as an erroneous attitude; and folly, he holds, is a suitable target for open and unequivocal ridicule. This the Clerk receives. Calling in the aid of the playful Muse, the poet for a time affects to agree with the Clerk's view of life, and facetiously describes how the devil is provoked into giving Jachin his special attention:

> No wonder Satan took the thing amiss,
> To be opposed by such a man as this—
> A man so grave, important, cautious, wise,
> Who dared not trust his feeling or his eyes;
> No wonder he should lurk and lie in wait,
> Should fit his hooks and ponder on his bait,
> Should on his movements keep a watchful eye;
> For he pursued a fish who led the fry.
> With his own peace our Clerk was not content,
> He tried, good man! to make his friends repent.

A little later the Clerk ('our saint') is described, in a somewhat Hudibrastic metaphor which links the religious with the military, as

> An interloper,—one who, out of place,
> Had volunteer'd upon the side of grace.

This is how Jachin appears to 'Satan's friends' among his acquaintance. They conspire to test him, hoping to discover frailty, but are worsted in the combat; 'the cup' and the 'artful lass' have no power to entice him from theological disputation. Crabbe, not yet wholly discarding his Hudibrastic metaphor, comments:

> They were indeed a weak, impatient set,
> But their shrewd prompter had his engines yet;
> Had various means to make a mortal trip,
> Who shunn'd a flowing bowl and rosy lip;
> And knew a thousand ways his heart to move,
> Who flies from banquets and who laughs at love.

Immediately afterwards the poet dismisses the playful Muse, for he holds that satirical treatment is appropriate only within clearly defined limits. It has to be

abandoned as soon as the boundary of distress and crime
is reached. The Parish Clerk's extravagant self-conceit
has been duly exposed as absurd. We are now to be
shown the stages of his moral ruin. In Crabbe's view,
since the moral ruin of a human being can never be
absurd, it ought to be contemplated with gravity, and
hence a different tone is required for its presentation
to the reader.

The poet seems to be prepared to sacrifice harmony
of tone in order to distribute his own kind of poetic
justice: the Clerk must receive the poetic treatment
consonant with his moral deserts. But in fact there is no
incongruity between the two parts of the story. The
tone is, indeed, modified in the second part, but it is not
precisely the kind of modification for which the author
seems to be preparing us. There is no further mockery
or facetiousness, but neither is there an abrupt transition to a tone of uniform solemnity. The apparently
non-committal manner of narrating incidents is maintained; it is the tone of Crabbe's interjections that most
markedly alters.

We are shown how Jachin persuades himself that his
virtue ought to receive a cash reward, how he forms a
plan of obtaining this reward by robbing the collection-
plate in church, how he determines to carry out the plan,
and (with much circumstantial detail, both material and
psychological) how he does carry it out many times,
maintaining a precarious belief in his own rectitude
until the very moment when his guilt is discovered.
The Clerk's attitude is still revealed mainly through his
own words—though with a difference. In the first part
of the poem Jachin erects, as it were, a verbal image of
his virtue for public exhibition. In the second part he

converses with himself.[1] Crabbe's chief concern in recording the debate that goes on in the Clerk's mind is to make us watch closely the successive stages of the man's moral disintegration as revealed first by his thoughts and then by the actions to which they lead.

Occasionally in the course of this narrative the author's own judgments on the Clerk are made evident; the tone in which they are expressed is noticeably different from the facetious mockery which characterises the passages quoted from the first part. Employing an oblique method of criticism, Crabbe describes Jachin's dissatisfaction with the low esteem in which he is held by the world:

> To this false judgment of the vulgar mind,
> He was not fully, as a saint, resign'd.

The censure here lies in the implied discrepancy between professed sainthood and authentic saintliness. The tone is scarcely grave, but the sardonic note is unlike the open ridicule of the earlier passages. Later there is a 'detachable' passage of grave moralising (still echoing the military metaphor):

> Alas! how often erring mortals keep
> The strongest watch against the foes who sleep;
> While the more wakeful, bold and artful foe
> Is suffer'd guardless and unmark'd to go.

And there is a sententious interjection:

> Fertile is evil in the soul of man.

[1] With the notable exception of a passage towards the end in which he explains to the 'pitying crowd' that, whilst he has earlier given himself out to be an example of virtue triumphing over Satan, his true significance is as an example of weakness and guilt.

This moral commonplace at the same time interprets the process that is taking place in the Parish Clerk's soul, and itself receives additional power and point from its context in the description of a particular instance of the fertility of evil.

It seems, then, that the playful Muse has lent her aid only in a few passages which, though conspicuous, are not of very great importance in determining the prevailing tones of the poem. The passages of explicit moralising do not contribute much more. The significant contrasts that are undoubtedly made in the course of the tale are primarily contrasts between moral facts, which dictate literary tone in a less obvious way. What matters is much less the presence or absence of a jesting tone than the discrimination and distinct revelation of the successive moral states of the Clerk as shown in his demeanour. I have already referred to the contrast between the Clerk's unctuous self-advertisement at the beginning of the tale and the passages of self-persuasion which come later. In the latter, the moral blindness or obtuseness already evident in the former manifests itself in a different way: not as a static condition but as a factor in a process, an agent co-operating with avarice to determine the conclusion of Jachin's reasoning. Both the profession of virtue and the interior debate are presented minutely. But in the first case the effect of the minuteness is to make us feel that the Clerk is overdoing his protestations; in the second, minute treatment is necessary to give us a full understanding of what is happening.

A contrast of a rather different order appears if we compare a couplet from the earlier part of the tale:

> By many a text he proved his doctrine sound,
> And look'd in triumph on the tempters round—

with one which occurs near the end:

> On the broad beach, the silent summer-day,
> Stretch'd on some wreck, he wore his life away.

Each couplet is representative of that part of the poem in which it appears. In both, the manner is scrupulously neutral and transparent; our first impression is simply one of matter-of-factness. But the first couplet is brisk and the second lingering: the former conveys the Clerk's assurance, the latter his despondency. This is brought about partly by the pace of the verse. In the first couplet each line can be read without a break; in the other both lines demand a pause in the middle, and are further protracted by long vowels. But even more important is the selection of material used in the two couplets. The former presents a social occasion (the Clerk ringed round with 'tempters' and holding his own). The latter emphasises his solitude—the human environment has been replaced by inanimate nature, including an object (the wreck) which, like the Clerk, has been abandoned by human beings. The adjectives 'broad' and 'silent' accentuate the solitude by contrast with the restricted and wordy scene conveyed in the first couplet. But only in a single word does the second couplet patently do more than state a simple fact: 'he *wore* his life away'. This conveys a moral and psychological fact in its metaphorical summing-up of Jachin's self-destruction by remorse; and it makes a biological statement too, for the Clerk has also to be seen as a living creature in decline. But in neither couplet is there any overt attempt to compel our response. The first does not direct us to condemn or deride, nor the latter to feel compassion. Crabbe exhibits images for our contemplation.

We can now see that the poet's dictum, 'There is no jesting with distress and crime', amounts to much more than a resolution to lay aside the facetious tone when a certain point in the story is reached. It is an assertion of the principle of proportion: feeling—and its expression—must be appropriate to the object.

That there is no jesting with crime is, of course, debatable, as we can see by looking at Pope's treatment of the career of Sir Balaam in the third Moral Essay. Here Pope describes a series of events which constitute something not unlike the career of the Parish Clerk, on a different scale and in a different social sphere. Balaam is 'A plain good man ... Religious, punctual, frugal'—he is a 'saint' in the same sense as Jachin. And, says Pope, 'The Dev'l was piqued such saintship to behold'. (Clearly, the story of the Parish Clerk would not have been altogether what it is if Crabbe had not read Pope.) But Pope maintains the same tone throughout the story: the criminality of Sir Balaam, who is damned by being made rich, is shown as ridiculous and grotesque. The poet is not in the least concerned with his distress. The story *is* a jest of a kind: a mordant jest embodying a perfectly serious and commendable piece of social and moral criticism. But Pope is careful to show Sir Balaam as a social and commercial being; we see him almost entirely from the outside. When we hear about the secret resolution with which he soothes his conscience—

'I'll now give sixpence where I gave a groat;
Where once I went to Church, I'll now go twice—
And so am clear too of all other vice—'

this strikes us as a justifiable piece of eavesdropping on Pope's part.[1] The tone of the whole passage is perfectly appropriate to Sir Balaam *as the author sees him*. But Crabbe views the Parish Clerk in a different light. He is primarily interested in Jachin's mind: we learn a good deal about his surroundings and his actions, but these are only significant through being seen in conjunction with the workings of his mind—Crabbe has tried to 'paint the features' of the Clerk's soul. A jesting tone would be irrelevant and incongruous not only in an analysis of the workings of a mind moving towards crime, but also in the account of the distress which follows his discovery. During the revelation of his heart and mind before this discovery he has become for us an individual, not a social or moral or psychological type. We expect to learn of his feelings after the discovery; and we do learn, though not so much from a description of them as from an account of his demeanour which enables us to deduce the distress from its outward signs.

'It has always', says Crabbe, 'been held as a salutary exercise of the mind, to contemplate the evils and miseries of our nature.'[2] Both Pope and Crabbe aim at exercising the reader's mind with salutary effect. But in Crabbe's tale the contemplation is not concentrated on *mores*; it penetrates further into nature.

The tale of the Parish Clerk may be said to illustrate

---

[1] *Cf.* these lines from *The Parish Clerk*:
    'The old and widows may their trifles miss,
    There must be evil in a good like this:
    But I'll be kind—the sick I'll visit twice,
    Where now but once, and freely give advice.'
[2] Prefatory note on Letter XXIII (*Prisons*), *The Borough*; *Works*, IV, p. 57.

the truth of Jeffrey's remark that, while the first fruits of observation are most commonly found to issue in satire, the satirist makes use of only half the discoveries of the observer, whereas the true result of observation should be not so much to cast down the proud as to raise the lowly. In *The Parish Clerk* we see the downfall of pride; but in a sense (though not in the sense Jeffrey intended) Jachin is subsequently 'raised'. For Crabbe does not leave us feeling that we have witnessed the end of an utterly insignificant person. It is true that he scrupulously avoids anything which might lead us to sentimentalise the Clerk. Our compassion must never overshadow our judgment—but the converse is also true. The poet is not intent on 'moral lessons' in any narrow sense. The moral lesson is indeed made explicit in the Clerk's own words to the crowd; but the tale ends in one of Crabbe's impressive 'moral silences'.[1] There is no moralising at all in the concluding lines, which well exemplify the poet's way of insisting, equally and simultaneously, on the homely and prosaic (the loft, the vicar's enquiry) and on the awe-inspiring (the utterly lonely death):

> He said, and saw no more the human face;
> To a lone loft he went, his dying place,
> And, as the vicar of his state inquired,
> Turn'd to the wall and silently expired!

[1] The frame of mind which Crabbe seems to try to induce in the reader by some of his more sombre tales is well suggested by a couplet in *Smugglers and Poachers* which describes the feelings of a party of men on discovering the bodies of two brothers, a poacher and a gamekeeper, who have killed each other:
> On all a momentary silence came,
> A common softness, and a moral shame.
>   (*Tales of the Hall*, XXI; *Works*, VII, p. 273).

IV

ORDER

I

CRABBE the younger imputes to his father an 'insensibility to the beauty of order' which prevents him from succeeding in the design of a poem as a whole. While admitting that there are many 'detached passages' in the poet's work which are well ordered, he remarks that the power of design can properly be judged only

in the conduct of the whole; in the selection of the subject and its amplifications; in the relative disposition and comparative prominency of the parts, and in the contrasts afforded by bearing lightly or heavily on the pencil.

And he adds: 'In these things Mr. Crabbe is generally admitted to be not a little deficient'.[1]

But it is unsatisfactory thus to judge Crabbe's work *en masse*. His peculiar proficiency, which is well worth defining, appears only in some of his poems. *The Parish Register* and *The Borough* certainly will not bear the application of the biographer's criterion. But in many of the tales there can be seen the successful functioning of a sense of form different from that which is shown in *The Library* and *The Village* (poems which met the conventional requirements of the poet's son quite well). The conflict between two conceptions of literary form constitutes a central factor in Crabbe's development.

[1] *Life*, pp. 165-6.

These may be roughly described as, first, design imposed on amorphous subject-matter, and second, an interaction between subject-matter and expression giving a literary structure that is congruous with the configuration of characters and events. The relation between these two conceptions, and the evolution of the later one, may be understood by considering the arrangement of complete works and the conduct of some of the tales.

The biographer praises *The Library* and *The Village* for being 'framed on a regular and classical plan,—perhaps, in that respect, they may be considered more complete and faultless than any of his later pieces'.[1] Yet these poems do not reveal a fine sense of *literary* order.

In *The Library*, between an introductory passage on the advantages to be gained from reading, and a conclusion asserting that the sorrows of authorship are but a part of the inevitable misfortune of life and should not discourage perseverance, the poet makes a survey of the contents of a library; the divisions (into divinity, philosophy, medicine, law, and so on) are such as a librarian might be expected to make. That is to say, the author makes use of a professional system of classification which conveniently pre-arranges his material for him.

The Village presented different, and partly fortuitous, problems. The arrangement of the first book is not the result of a superimposed pattern, but arises naturally from the author's theme. He asserts that 'the real Picture of the Poor' ought to be shown, exposes the falsehoods of pastoral verse, and describes the actual miseries of contemporary villagers. So far the plan is

[1] *Life*, p. 121.

'regular' enough. But it is hard to understand how the poet's son can have found the work as a whole 'complete and faultless' in plan. The ostensible purpose of the second book is to forestall the criticism that the poet has omitted the consolations of village life. Most of the book, however, appears to have been written as a pretext for introducing a panegyric on Lord Robert Manners (running to nearly a hundred lines) into a poem with the original theme of which he has no connection whatsoever. Crabbe, indeed, tells us that he had written some verses to the memory of Manners at about the time (early in 1783) when Dr. Johnson saw the manuscript of *The Village*, and that, on Johnson's objecting to the proposed dedication, these verses, 'by a junction, it is presumed, not forced or unnatural', were made to form the concluding part of the poem.[1] But the junction, only too evidently, *is* forced, and violence has been done to the 'regular and classical plan'.

The Address to the Reader prefixed to *The Newspaper* makes it clear that Crabbe knows this poem is not a satisfactory whole, though he trusts that his manipulation of the parts holds it together well enough. At first, he says, he intended to write only a few lines describing 'that variety of dissociating articles which are huddled together in our Daily Papers', but later 'conceived that this might be done methodically, and with some connection of parts, by taking a larger scope; which notwithstanding I have done, I must still apologise for a want of union and coherence in my poem. Subjects like this will not easily admit of them: we cannot slide from theme to theme in an easy and graceful succession; but, on quitting one thought, there will be an unavoidable

---

[1] *Works*, II, p. 13, n. 1.

hiatus, and in general an awkward transition into that which follows'.[1] This is true—but do union and coherence consist in no more than a mastery of the art of transition and the choice of a subject which permits a sliding from theme to theme in an easy and graceful succession? So Crabbe seems to have believed when he wrote *The Newspaper*.

By the time he wrote *The Parish Register* he gave far less attention to ease of transition. Here the transitions are as abrupt as they well could be. 'Next died *the Widow Goe*. . . . Next died the LADY who yon Hall possess'd. . . . Then died a Rambler.' Almost any individual sketch could be removed without impairing the plan—adequately described by Jeffrey as 'very simple but singular'. There is a general account of village manners, illustrated by descriptions, first of the cottage of a frugal villager, then of a group of improvident poor; there follows a series of portraits of individuals, representing 'all the remarkable baptisms, marriages, and funerals, that appear in [the] register for the preceding year'. The specimens are arranged in the simplest possible way, but there is little artistic cohesion. Considering the material, it is difficult to see what better arrangement could have been made. The poem derives what unity it has from the homogeneous tone in which its theme is treated; but the structure is very loose—it is an aggregation rather than a structure. It is, indeed, an aggregation of units, many of which are, in themselves, well formed; Crabbe himself invites us to accept the poem as a gallery of pictures:

> These are our groups; our Portraits next appear,
> And close our Exhibition for the year.

[1] *Works*, II, p. 111.

Still, though groups and portraits are works of art, an exhibition is not a composite work of art.

So straggling and amorphous a subject as that of *The Borough* cannot easily be given coherence—its unity is merely topographical. The fairly homogeneous tone of the work has, as has been remarked, a certain unifying effect. Yet *The Borough* is even less satisfactorily ordered than *The Parish Register*, in which the manner of treating the component parts confers on the collection at least the kind of affinity that exists between various pictures of human beings. *The Borough* is a medley of descriptions, portraits, reflections, anecdotes and tales—more of a medley than the letter-headings suggest, since many letters are miscellaneous in content.

Crabbe has relied largely on the appeal of variety to satisfy readers of this work—a 'variety of relations, characters, and descriptions'. He could have excused his neglect of design by an appeal to the authority of Dr. Johnson, who wrote of Pope's *Windsor Forest*:

The objection made by Dennis is the want of plan, of a regular subordination of parts terminating in the principal and original design. There is this want in most descriptive poems, because as the scenes, which they must exhibit successively, are all subsisting at the same time, the order in which they are shewn must by necessity be arbitrary, and more is not to be expected from the last part than from the first. The attention, therefore, which cannot be detained by suspense, must be excited by diversity.[1]

But although the order of scenes in *The Borough* must by necessity be arbitrary, some order there had to be. As in *The Library*, so in *The Borough*, the arrangement of material is determined by non-poetic considerations.

[1] *Lives of the English Poets*, ed. G. Birkbeck Hill (1905), vol. 3, p. 225. But see below, Chapter V.

Crabbe pretends that a friend living in the country has invited him to describe the Borough, and he writes a number of descriptive letters. The general description is followed by an account of the Church, and the next three letters relate to the religious and political life of the town. Having thus disposed of Church and State, the poet turns to occupations, grading them according to social prestige: professions take precedence of trades. As work is followed by play, he passes on to amusements and recreations (Letters IX-XII). The contents of Letters XIII-XXII fall within the categories of charity and poverty. By a sufficiently natural transition we proceed to prisons in Letter XXIII, and we conclude (not without surprise) with a Letter on schools. This is perhaps placed at the end because the theme of study links the scholar with the poet, and Crabbe is able without difficulty to make his transition to the account of the poet who portrays 'Man as he is'—the author's apologia. The letter-titles suggest that Crabbe has devised a number of compartments into which a vast quantity of varied material may be sorted; closer inspection shows how rough the sorting has been. In retrospect, the work assumes a certain coherence, but this is unrelated to considerations of design.

After reading *The Borough*, Jeffrey advised Crabbe to 'apply his great powers to the construction of some interesting and connected story'. This was the best piece of advice he ever gave the poet; and Crabbe took it. But in doing so he was not striking out in an entirely new direction; he had already written some successful tales in verse.

He did not at once understand what kind of narrative Jeffrey wanted. The critic later explained that

what he had meant was that he would welcome more
tales like *Sir Eustace Grey* and *The Hall of Justice*. But
Crabbe not unnaturally supposed that a very long tale
was desired—'if not an Epic Poem, strictly so denominated, yet such composition as would possess a
regular succession of events, and a catastrophe to which
every incident should be subservient, and which every
character, in a greater or lesser degree, should conspire
to accomplish'.[1]

No doubt his attempts to write novels had taught him
the difficulty of devising a complex but unified action,
and he had little hope of surmounting the difficulty in a
large-scale poem. He compares the principal and inferior characters in such a poem to a general and his
army, each pursuing his adventures 'in unison with the
movements and purposes of the whole body'; he saw
the necessity for 'such distribution of persons and
events'—but also saw that it was not for him to attempt
it. 'I found myself obliged,' he writes, 'to relinquish
an undertaking, for which the characters I could
command, and the adventures I could describe, were
altogether unfitted.'[2]

But some characters and some events he knew he
could describe. And even though the characters at his
disposal would not coalesce into one body, they were
not an unconnected multitude, but 'beings of whom
might be formed groups and smaller societies'. Tales
of the kind he could accomplish bore, 'in points of connection and importance', the same relation to the
Heroic Poem as bands of pilgrims, tourists or adven-
turers to a regular and disciplined army. Crabbe was

[1] *Works*, IV, p. 137 (Preface to the *Tales*).
[2] *Ibid*. pp. 137-8.

aware that in producing a collection of tales he lost much 'for want of unity of subject and grandeur of design', but believed he gained something 'by greater variety of incident and more minute display of character, by accuracy of description and diversity of scene'.

The staple of any work, therefore, which would allow the freest exercise of his distinctive power must be the brief tale, taking in a small number of characters and a comparatively simple chain of events. But while recognising this fact, Crabbe was still seeking for some device for connecting the tales, some master-framework to enclose them all. This device would need to be less naïve than those he had already used—the clergyman turning over the pages of his parish register, or the letter-writing burgess. He was willing to learn from approved models how dissimilar tales might be united by 'some associating circumstance to which the whole number might bear equal affinity'. But neither Chaucer nor Boccaccio was of much help. Chaucer made him realise the difficulty of assigning each tale to a narrator appropriate both to that tale and to his companions in the band of story-tellers; but there was a further difficulty, for even if the mediaeval pilgrimage 'excused' the association of the Knight and Prioress with a drunken Miller, no enterprise in his own day would provide so heterogeneous a group. Boccaccio had avoided the first difficulty by giving his narrators no marked character; but it would have been pointless to imitate him in this.

The *Tales* of 1812, therefore, were submitted to the public 'connected by no other circumstance than their being productions of the same author, and devoted to the same purpose, the entertainment of his readers'.

Homogeneity of tone, scope and purpose is once again the principal factor which unifies the whole work. Instead of a collection of portraits we have a collection of stories.

But Crabbe still wished to solve the problem he had shelved. In his *Tales of the Hall* he arrives at a curious and characteristic solution which, whatever its defects, is not vulnerable to the objections he himself had raised against *The Canterbury Tales*. The link-story which provides the necessary 'associating circumstance' is a work of sober-toned verisimilitude. Two half-brothers meet, after years of separation, at the home of the elder and richer; the visit and its happy conclusion are described. The bulk of the work consists of life-stories in retrospect, inset in this narrative: the brothers recount the adventures which came their way before they reached an unadventurous middle age; and there are also stories about other people, chiefly local residents, most of these stories being introduced by the prosy elder brother, with some help from the affable rector.

Thus summarised, the scheme of *Tales of the Hall* appears ungainly and simple to the point of naïveté. But it has certain notable advantages beyond that of serving as a convenient framework for the minor narratives. The link-story provides significant contrasts and correspondences with the inset tales. The material set forth in it is drawn from the same social stratum as that of most of the tales; but the events it records are much less striking than those in the insets. In the former all is quiet; there is enough activity to prevent a sense of the utterly static, but the happenings are of that trivial order which finds no place in a tale recounting some crisis in a life. The link-story reproduces the commonplace existence of every day faithfully. And yet the minor tensions of life and their resolution play an important part here: for example, the initial wariness of the two brothers and its disappearance; the cool draughts of suspicion or uncertainty which occasionally threaten their cordiality; the alternation of the younger brother's wish to rejoin his family with his contentment in his brother's company; his fear that he may have outstayed his welcome; his rueful feelings over the rector's too casual farewell. What at first sight appears as monochrome is seen on closer inspection to be variegated. Daily life, put under Crabbe's microscope, reveals patterns and undulations of feeling not altogether unlike those which form the themes of the more arresting narratives; but because the scale is different the feelings called into play are milder in the link-story. And it is not only that everyday events are trivial and everyday emotions undisturbing; it is also that Crabbe enacts the experience of the brothers at a very different pace from that of the inset tales. These tales may present sequences of events extending over a number of years; we take a foreshortened view of them, in which only the most important moments count. In at least some parts of the link-story we witness the passage of time almost to the accompaniment of a clock's soporific ticking. Crabbe thus expresses the restfulness of everyday life—the life, at least, of elderly people who possess adequate means —and the link-story provides a norm of existence to which we return, with a certain relief, at the end of each tale:

> Now all is quiet, and the mind sustains
> Its proper comforts, its befitting pains;
> The heart reposes.[1]

[1] *The Old Bachelor* (*Tales of the Hall*, X); *Works*, VI, p. 250.

To recapitulate: Crabbe's poetry up to and including *The Borough* bears witness both to his awareness of the amorphous nature of his subject-matter (at least *en masse*) and to his sense of the need for design. His powers of observation, analysis and classification provide him with material, and enable him to sort it out, to some extent. But, as we have seen, the form of the poems in which this material is incorporated is not determined by the material; there is no effectual interaction between poetic design and embodied material. Crabbe tries to arrive at a workable scheme. He has studied the rules of composition: invention, disposition and elocution are in his mind—as literary proprieties rather than as guiding principles; he knows, for instance, the importance of transition, but appears to believe that an ingenious writer can quite properly contrive transitions between subjects not in themselves connected.

His interest lies rather in displaying his subject than in the evolution of design. It would not be unjust to conclude, on the evidence of the first half of his writings, that he regarded design as, largely, contrivance. The only large-scale work in which contrivance is united with the power to exploit the suggestions about literary form offered by the material is *Tales of the Hall*. Even here, as he approaches the writing of this work, Crabbe has in mind a literary problem in which the form of the poem is still regarded as something to be contrived: How can dissociated elements be combined by some associating circumstance to which all the elements bear the same affinity? The *conscious* purpose is still to impose, rather than to elicit, order. But in the working-out of his design he realises (though in a fumbling way) the formal potentialities lying in the differences of pace, mood and scale between the link-story and the inset narratives. *Tales of the Hall* thus represents the somewhat uneasy co-operation of two conceptions of form.

II

By the time he wrote *Tales of the Hall* Crabbe was already expert in narrative verse. It is in his short tales that the form of the material best harmonises with, and helps to determine, that of the literary form.

Clearly, narrative corresponds better than descriptive writing with the poet's interest in human beings, which is chiefly in their growth and development. Crabbe's principal aim in his tales is to show, with the greatest possible actuality and clarity, what he considers most significant in this or that character as manifested in a series of events. He represents selected traits of character, and scenes and events which are chosen from a whole life-history because it is precisely these that best mark the course of development taken by the peculiar traits of character which constitute the *motif* of the poem.

He worked his way towards this kind of writing gradually, as he came to see what he could do best. His progress here may be seen as a concern with contrast developing into a concern with process—the latter, indeed, never supersedes the former, but significantly supplements it.

Crabbe's concern with contrast shows itself in many different ways. But the relevant question to ask when we are considering the evolution of his short verse tales is, whether the contrasted entities exist at the same time or successively. The principal contrast drawn in *The Vil-*

lage is between the falsehood of conventional pastoral poetry and the facts of rural life; that in the first few pages of *The Parish Register* is between two groups of persons whose prototypes could be observed in actuality. In both cases the things or people contrasted exist at the same time: poets are writing pastoral poetry while village life is as Crabbe describes it; good and bad villagers live side by side. No question of succession in time arises. But as soon as the poet begins to concern himself with contrasts between different states of the same character, or different phases in a character's fortunes, he is already thinking in terms of process to some extent. A tendency to think in these terms can be seen even in the early work. *The Village* contains a sketch of the typical pattern to be seen in the fortunes of a poor villager from youth to old age; while some of the portraits in *The Parish Register* (those of Roger Cuff, Richard Monday and the Widow Goe, for instance) reveal development of character or progression of events, or both.

How description or portraiture in Crabbe aspires towards narrative may be clearly seen in the lines on Phoebe Dawson in *The Parish Register*; the two antithetical sketches of Phoebe—first as the 'sweetest flower' of the village, next as 'this child of weakness, want, and care'—may be static pictures, but they represent two phases in her fortunes. A similar method is used, much later, in *The Lover's Journey* (*Tales*, X), where there are three pictures of dissimilar states of mind, giving us the three distinctive phases in a process occupying only a few hours. However, the emphasis in both instances is rather on pointing the contrast than on delineating the process.

The poet has thus described his two chief modes of viewing the life of an individual:

> Minutely trace man's life; year after year,
> Through all his days let all his deeds appear,
> And then, though some may in that life be strange,
> Yet there appears no vast nor sudden change:
> The links that bind the various deeds are seen,
> And no mysterious void is left between.
>
> But let these binding links be all destroy'd,
> All that through years he suffer'd or enjoy'd:
> Let that vast gap be made, and then behold—
> This was the youth, and he is thus when old;
> Then we at once the work of time survey,
> And in an instant see a life's decay;
> Pain mix'd with pity in our bosoms rise,
> And sorrow takes new sadness from surprise.[1]

Crabbe prefers as a rule to combine these two modes, and, when his treatment is minute, he aims at showing the significant links which 'bind the various deeds', since an all-inclusive account, even if it were possible, could not be a work of art. There is a skilful combination of contrast and process in *Procrastination* (*Tales*, IV). This tale is based on the contrast between a farewell and a return. The lovers, Dinah and Rupert, say goodbye with great warmth of feeling when Rupert leaves home in the hope of making his fortune. On his return, years later, he is coldly received by Dinah, whose heart is now engrossed by the wealth she has inherited from her aunt. But the tale consists of more than two contrasted scenes. While Rupert is away (and during this period *his* feelings do not change) we are shown that gradual development of Dinah's avarice (she felt her

[1] Opening lines of *The Parting Hour* (*Tales*, II); *Works*, IV, pp. 175-6.

passion for a shilling grow') which prepares us for
what will happen when Rupert returns. When the expected companion-picture is displayed, it clearly marks
the extent of the change in Dinah (warmth of feeling
being used as an index to her character) and 'places'
this change by recording the sudden disenchantment of
Rupert. Here, then, pictures of dissimilar phases in the
relationship between two characters are significantly
linked by the description of a process.[1]

For an author who wishes to describe or enact a
process, the power of making and expressing distinctions
is even more important than that of observing and expressing contrasts. His concern is with the gradual. We
may say, perhaps, that Crabbe the naturalist makes the
distinctions between the different phases of a process,
while Crabbe the poet expresses them. But the naturalist
discovers more than the poet can use, for not all aspects
of human life are intrinsically suitable for rendering in a
verse tale.

The problem which the poet faced may be more
clearly realised if we examine it in the light of Bagehot's
remarks on the 'literatesque':

There should be a word in the language of literary art to express
what the word 'picturesque' expresses for the fine arts. *Picturesque*
means fit to be put into a picture; we want a word *literatesque*,
'fit to be put into a book'. . . .

. . . The word '*literatesque*' would mean, if we possessed it,
that perfect combination in the *subject-matter* of literature,

[1] Crabbe never abandoned the simpler procedure of dealing with
life-stories by means of contrasted portraits. In the series of tales, *Farewell and Return* (*Posthumous Tales*, VI-XXII; *Works*, VIII), each tale
presents a contrast between the earlier and later states of characters
or places.

which suits the *art* of literature. . . . There are the infinite number of classes of human beings, but in each of these classes there is a distinctive type which, if we could expand it out in words, would define the class. We cannot expand it in formal terms any more than a landscape or a species of landscape; but we have an art, an art of words, which can draw it. Travellers and others often bring home, in addition to their long journals— which though so living to them, are so dead, so inanimate, so un-descriptive to all else—a pen-and-ink sketch, rudely done very likely, but which, perhaps, even the more for the blots and strokes, gives a distinct notion, an emphatic image, to all who see it. They say at once, *now* we know the sort of thing. The sketch has *hit* the mind. True literature does the same. It describes sorts, varieties, and permutations, by delineating the type of each sort, the ideal of each variety, the central, marking trait of each permutation.

. . . the business of the poet, of the artist, is with *types*; and those types are mirrored in reality . . . the poet must find in that reality, the *literatesque* man, the *literatesque* scene which nature intends for him, and which will live in his page.[1]

What constitutes a type for Crabbe the story-teller is a process involving one or more human beings and embodying the development and operation of some passion or affection. Both conditions have to be fulfilled. Character in action is not significant unless it manifests a passion or a moral quality; on the other hand, the passion or quality is defined by the action, and we are not required to entertain any conception of, say, resentment or conscience or procrastination in the abstract.[2]

Crabbe's stories, however, do not always embody literatesque types. It is not that, like Jeffrey, we find

[1] 'Wordsworth, Tennyson, and Browning; or, Pure, Ornate and Grotesque Art in English Poetry', *Literary Studies*, Everyman ed. (1944), II, pp. 308-11.

[2] A concern with 'types' in this sense does not in any way preclude the incorporation of individualising traits.

the material used in some of the tales 'disgusting', on the ground that the characters described are depraved and abject and therefore 'have no hold upon any of the feelings that lead us to take an interest in our fellow-creatures'. It is that the material may strike us as artistically useless. The character and adventures of Frederick Thompson (*The Borough*, Letter XII, *Players*) may be *representative*; but the character is indistinct and the episodes are strung together with no necessary sequence. The story does not amount to the delineation of a type in Bagehot's sense of the word; there seems to be a fault in the selection of material.

But besides this, it is clear that a literatesque theme, possessing 'that perfect combination in the *subject-matter* of literature, which suits the *art* of literature', must receive fit handling from the author if an 'emphatic image' is to be created. In Crabbe's phrase, the conduct of the poem must be 'judiciously managed'. Failures among this poet's tales are more often the result of injudicious management than of a lack of literatesqueness in the subject. Paradoxically, some of Crabbe's most powerful tales are partial failures.

Villars (*Posthumous Tales*, V) shows how a highly literatesque theme, excellently handled for the most part, may be marred by a feeble conclusion. For a long time Villars loves without success a woman who favours another suitor. When this rival proves to be a trifler, the woman, disenchanted, marries Villars; but on the lover's reappearance her former love revives, and Villars returns from a visit to Ireland to find that his wife has left him. His sole passion thenceforth is revenge: he will recapture his wife, and the two will spend the remainder of their lives performing a kind of joint penance, she for wantonness, and he for vengefulness, in an isolated house which he has chosen for that purpose. Villars's fears, his dismay on finding his wife gone, the completeness with which the desire to punish her dominates his thoughts, the elaborate care with which his scheme is laid, the desolate appearance and situation of the house—all these are powerfully set before us. At length Villars discovers his wife, carries her off and drives 'madly' away towards the deserted mansion:

> All in that ruin Villars had prepared,
> And meant her fate and sorrow to have shared;
> There he design'd they should for ever dwell,
> The weeping pair of a monastic cell. . . .
>
> And all was order'd in his mind—the pain
> He must inflict, the shame she must sustain;
> But such his gentle spirit, such his love,
> The proof might fail of all he meant to prove.

Having thus prepared us for a climax, Crabbe gives us the following lines:

> Features so dear had still maintain'd their sway,
> And looks so loved had taught him to obey;
> Rage and Revenge had yielded to the sight
> Of charms that waken wonder and delight;
> The harsher passions from the heart had flown,
> And LOVE regain'd his Subject and his Throne.

Evidently the poet had in mind a sudden revulsion of feeling. This could have been brought out in the briefest of scenes presenting the arrival of Villars and his wife at the lonely mansion; but we are only *told* what happens—we do not see or feel it happening. Crabbe often adds to a concluding scene a passage dwelling on its significance, and these interpretative passages may well strike us as inessential appendages; but at the end of *Villars* we have the appendage without the vital 'scene'. There is nothing that hits the mind.

In *Smugglers and Poachers* (*Tales of the Hall*, XXI) the material, again, seems literatesque enough. But although it suits the art of literature it scarcely suits the art of the brief tale. We need to know a good deal about the early lives of the two brothers, and to have in mind the contrast of character between the two boys, in order to understand fully the nature of the conflict which arises between them in manhood, when they are rivals not only in love but in occupation (the elder a conscientious but merciless gamekeeper, the younger a brave but reckless smuggler and poacher). The first part of the story is excessively bare: it consists of a recital of facts and an emphatic pointing of contrasts, but Crabbe has time only to tell us about the brothers, not to show them to us in a sufficiently circumstantial social context and with a sufficient filling-out of character. Nevertheless, he is magnificent when he reaches the crucial part of the action and presents, with the amplitude they need, those episodes which show how the rivalry of the brothers leads to their death and the unhappiness of the woman whom both love.

There is a certain misshapenness also about *Sir Owen Dale* (*Tales of the Hall*, XII). The Rector tells the tale of this local worthy who, repulsed by a coquette, seeks to be revenged by extracting from his nephew a promise to win her love and then jilt her. The nephew performs the first part of the promise but, having meantime fallen in love with the lady, begs to be released from the remainder. Sir Owen refuses for a time, but is at length brought to relent by hearing from the lips of one of his tenants a story of revenge turned to forgiveness by the husband's witnessing the poverty and misery of the unfaithful wife and her lover. The 'inset' story is by far the more considerable; that of Sir Owen himself strains our belief to no purpose, even though the character of Sir Owen is firmly drawn. It is not difficult to see why Crabbe should have arranged matters as he did. The tenant's confidant had to be a man disappointed in love and ardently desiring revenge, in order to elicit from the speaker so full and impassioned an account of the evolution of his fortunes and feelings; but none of the three principal story-tellers in *Tales of the Hall* could properly be made to serve this purpose. In order, therefore, to preserve verisimilitude, Crabbe gives us a story-within-a-story-within-a-story; but the impression of *Sir Owen Dale* that remains with us is rather that of a double revenge-story somewhat resembling a pair of Siamese twins.

So much for Crabbe's half-successes. He has also left many tales in which the process which constitutes the theme not only is literatesque in itself but also receives consistently competent expression in literary form. Some of the well-managed tales, it is true, are of small stature poetically. *The Wager* (*Tales*, XVIII) typifies fairly those tales which attain competence without any special significance: the exposition of character and situation is straightforward and brisk; and, while no *development* of character is involved, the action advances towards a character-*revealing* conclusion which the exposition would not lead us to expect, but which, by the time it is reached, is felt to be the natural reaction of *these* characters to *these* circumstances. Even among the more considerable tales, not every one gives such striking proof of the author's actualising power as does *Villars* or the last half of *Smugglers and Poachers*. Crabbe's liking for 'uncoloured' themes often finds expression in work whose merits, necessarily, are not of an arresting kind. In *The Brothers* (*Tales*, XX) he develops a theme of this nature in a leisurely way, showing us the generosity of a sailor towards his cold, egoistic brother, the sailor's return as a cripple, and his brother's ingratitude, manifesting itself in a series of heartless actions which, by degrees, deprive the cripple of every source of comfort and satisfaction. The merit here lies in the measured gradualness with which the action unfolds, each event after the sailor's return to his brother compelling the former to penetrate further behind his brother's mask of kindness, and the latter to make increasingly strenuous efforts at self-deception in defence of a complacency which, finally shattered by the sailor's death, gives place to a futile remorse.

More striking among Crabbe's successes are *Resentment* (*Tales*, XVII) and *Delay has Danger* (*Tales of the Hall*, XIII). They do not show greater power than the three half-successes discussed earlier, but they do show better judgment and a livelier sense of proportion in the use of this power.[1] They are, moreover, worth looking at closely for another reason: they show that Crabbe's ability to depict process in a satisfactory literary form

[1] The following seem to me to be no less successful: *Peter Grimes* (*The Borough*, XXII), *Edward Shore* (*Tales*, XI), *The Mother* (*Tales*, VIII), *Jesse and Colin* (*Tales*, XIII), *The Confidant* (*Tales*, XVI), *The Frank Courtship* (*Tales*, VI) and *Ruth* (*Tales of the Hall*, V). A reading of these tales should give a fair idea of the variety of merit and method to be found in Crabbe's narrative poems.

Mr. E. M. Forster writes on *Peter Grimes* in an essay in *Two Cheers for Democracy* (pp. 178-92); Mr. Arthur Sale discusses the structure of *The Confidant* in the article mentioned above, p. 14.

reveals itself notably in his varying modes of treating
the passage of time. His favourite method, well ex-
emplified in *Resentment*, consists of a 'timeless' or
static exposition, followed by a series of significant
'scenes' linked by compressed and laconic narrative,
the story proper ending in a 'scene'. It is in this
respect that the poet does something corresponding to
the younger Crabbe's demand for 'the contrasts afforded
by bearing lightly or heavily on the pencil'.

But the metaphor needs to be transposed from the
spatial to the temporal—the more so because the
spatial metaphor carries no suggestion of the importance of the increase of tension through the whole tale.
This increase is not brought about at an even rate. It
will be found as a rule that the tension is stronger in
the scenes than in the connecting narrative, and
strongest of all in scenes (usually occurring towards the
end of the tale) in which Crabbe makes his reader
aware of the moment-by-moment passage of time. The
first hundred lines or so of a tale are generally lacking
in tension, and they abound in precise circumstantial
detail of character and social setting, as well as of the
personal situation from which the action is to spring.[1]
The subsequent mixture of scene or soliloquy with narrative provides an alternate heightening and partial relaxation of tension. The later scenes, from which Crabbe
excludes everything not immediately relevant to that
part of the action, only make their full impact on a mind
which has retained the store of detail given earlier in

[1] Mr. Forster speaks of the 'flats' of *Peter Grimes*—'using "flats"
in no derogatory sense, but to indicate the glassy or muddy surface upon
which the action now proceeds and through which at any moment
something unexpected may emerge'. Both *Resentment* and *Delay has
Danger* have their 'flats' in this sense.

the poem. To change the previous metaphor, Crabbe focuses our attention, as we grow progressively better informed, on smaller and still smaller tracts of experience, with correspondingly greater actualisation. It is in the later stages of a tale that he most often succeeds in making his creations 'present in the mind'.

In the first part of *Resentment* we are not aware of the clock, or even of the calendar. Crabbe sets before us, in sufficiently copious detail, the characters, status, and way of life of the merchant Paul and of a worthy, staid lady living in the same town. These character-sketches are provisional. That of the lady is true as far as it goes; but it is incomplete and the tale expands it. The picture of the merchant represents the impression the world has of him; it is to be corrected later. After prudent deliberation the pair marry, and for an unspecified period enjoy an apparently secure mode of life. Then follows a brief but important scene in which, by inducing his unsuspecting wife to sign a document, the import of which she does not think it necessary to enquire about, the 'grave impostor' obtains her money in the hope of saving himself from bankruptcy. His financial ruin nevertheless follows, and Crabbe describes the demeanour of the husband and wife, both reduced to utter want. The husband is penitent in vain; his wife, though patient in enduring hardship, is filled with the bitterest resentment towards him. Crabbe is more informative about the wife, for from now on she is to be the active character, and her husband the passive. In all this part of the story the poet is working with foreshortened time, as it were, and exactitude about years and months is unnecessary.

The passion of resentment has now been implanted

in the wife, but although it thrives it cannot bear the fruit by which we are to know it fully, in the form of some decisive action or inaction, until husband and wife meet again. A fresh phase is reached when the wife, after inheriting a new fortune from a philanthropic cousin, returns to her 'ancient residence', now styling herself a widow, and devotes her time and wealth to sympathetic and systematic almsgiving. After some years the husband, unknown to her, wanders back to the same town, where he makes a precarious living by selling grit which he gets from a mason's yard. On a distant view of him as he drives his 'burthen'd ass' along the street, she judges the 'poor old man' a suitable object of charity, but when she learns who he is she considers 'the wretch' disqualified:

'Is this his lot?—but let him, let him feel—
Who wants the courage, not the will, to steal.'

Genuinely bountiful towards the neglected poor, she is implacable in denying charity to her husband. In this part of the tale her dominant passion—indeed, her sole *passion*—of resentment is sharply accentuated by a contrast which the opening lines of the story have laid before us in general terms, and which we now see embodied in two specific characters, those of mistress and servant. For the servant, Susan, like her mistress, has been brought to poverty in the past by her husband, but has nevertheless always been capable of free forgiveness. From now on, Crabbe makes us keep all three characters in view, the two women in the foreground and the man seen at a distance.

In the final episode (which occupies nearly a third of the tale) the poet gives us the fruit of resentment in all its bitter destructiveness. It is now that he begins to make us keenly conscious of the passage of time, first by specifying a season, and then by focusing our attention on one particular day. We are shown the old man contending with the cold:

> A dreadful winter came, each day severe,
> Misty when mild, and icy cold when clear;
> And still the humble dealer took his load,
> Returning slow, and shivering on the road.

We guess that he will die unless his wife relents at once. But

> The Lady, still relentless, saw him come,
> And said—'I wonder, has the wretch a home?'

This is the last that the poet, speaking in his own person, tells us about the old man. The rest we see through the pitying eyes of the companion. As she and her mistress watch him pass by the house a terse, trenchant dialogue takes place. The wife, energetic in self-justification and eloquent in denouncing her husband's misdeeds, is as far from ignoring his misery as from alleviating it. For the companion, on the other hand, while she admits his guilt, the spectacle of extreme suffering obliterates all other considerations:

> 'The snow,' quoth Susan, 'falls upon his bed—
> It blows beside the thatch—it melts upon his head.'—
> ''Tis weakness, child, for grieving guilt to feel:'—
> 'Yes, but he never sees a wholesome meal;
> Through his bare dress appears his shrivell'd skin,
> And ill he fares without, and worse within.'

Susan's descriptions of his predicament, homely, concrete and direct, constitute in themselves the most urgent appeals for humane action and drive home at the same time his want of the barest necessities of life and the very simple means by which he could be relieved.[1] The function of these descriptions is not to provide a single picture, increasingly elaborated, but to give us a narrative sequence in which the old man struggles through the snow and wind and is followed by the eye of imagination to his cold hut; his journey home and the women's talk about him proceed simultaneously. To each of Susan's appeals the Lady opposes some maxim of a wintry morality:

> 'Know you his conduct?'—'Yes, indeed, I know—
> And how he wanders in the wind and snow:
> Safe in our rooms the threat'ning storm we hear,
> But he feels strongly what we faintly fear.'
> 'Wilful was rich, and he the storm defied;
> Wilful is poor, and must the storm abide;'
> Said the stern Lady—''Tis in vain to feel.'

And Susan is sent off to her cooking. But the wife, seized by belated misgivings, calls her back and announces that she intends to provide her husband with sustenance—and nothing more. Susan is despatched with food, wine and a stonily righteous message:

> 'But, this inform him, that it is not love
> That prompts my heart, that duties only move.'

During her companion's absence the Lady occupies herself with a 'pious book' and with

> long musing on the chilling scene
> So lately past—the frost and sleet so keen—
> The man's whole misery in a single view—

until 'she could think some pity was his due'.

---

[1] *Cf.* one of the mottoes of the tale, taken from *King Lear*:
> 'How dost? . . . Art cold?
> I'm cold myself—Where is this straw, my fellow?
> The art of our necessities is strange,
> That can make vile things precious.'

On Susan's return, however, it appears that while the wife has been moralising, the husband has been dying:

> 'Dead!' said the startled Lady. 'Yes, he fell
> Close at the door where he was wont to dwell;
> There his sole friend, the Ass, was standing by,
> Half dead himself, to see his Master die.'

The Lady, still sensitive about her rectitude, entreats her companion not to blame her—a needless request, since the compassionate Susan is accusing her own heart instead.

Crabbe adds no comment. This would be superfluous, for he has already done completely what he set out to do. He has made an image of resentment, its characteristics standing out all the more clearly through its juxtaposition, in the later part of the story, with an image of forgiveness. He has first described the kind of nature in which resentment most readily takes root, and then recorded the means by which it may be implanted. But he is much more concerned to make us perceive its growth and, most of all, its fruit; and these are presented in such a way that the crucial stages in the evolution of the passion are enacted rather than merely described or related.

Given the wife's character and her sense of grievance against her husband, the catastrophe is all but inevitable when once the circumstances which make it possible have arisen; and our attention is focused with especial care on that brief period after these circumstances have arisen. The conclusion of *Delay has Danger* —the loss of the hero's betrothed—seems scarcely more avoidable, given the character of the hero and the circumstances in which he happens to be placed. Crabbe prepares us for this in his preamble:

Frail was the hero of my tale, but still
Was rather drawn by accident than will;
Some without meaning into guilt advance,
From want of guard, from vanity, from chance.

Here, as in *Resentment*, the poet is dealing with a process which ends in calamity because decisive action is delayed. But in *Resentment* it is only in the final episode that the danger of delay has to be felt; when this factor does operate, it operates suddenly and powerfully. This is not so in the other tale, in which, as soon as the initial situation suffers its first complication, delay is dangerous. A very different kind of process, therefore, forms the theme of *Delay has Danger*; and our attention is directed more upon the process than upon the calamity itself. It is, moreover, a gradual, unhurried process, which finds its wholly appropriate embodiment in a tale where the interest is diffused with remarkable evenness through several successive phases; these merge into each other almost imperceptibly, so that the tension grows very slowly, but also very surely. Crabbe shows us a man who supposes himself to be in an almost unchanging situation of which he is master, only to discover too late that he has been blind to the real situation and to the characters of the people involved, including his own. The situation has mastered him.

The peculiar quality of *Delay has Danger* can only be brought out with the help of a somewhat long summary. Henry, betrothed to Cecilia, is sent by his father to visit a noble patron during the interval between betrothal and wedding. Cecilia 'liked it not', but 'believed him faithful, though untried'. The youth is willing enough to return when a month has passed, but his father commands him to remain where he is in order to cultivate the patron's good graces still further. Henry, meanwhile, passes his time in a correctly loverlike way:

> In all his walks, in hilly heath or wood,
> Cecilia's form the pensive youth pursued;
> In the gray morning, in the silent noon,
> In the soft twilight, by the sober moon,
> In those forsaken rooms, in that immense saloon;
> And he, now fond of that seclusion grown,
> There reads her letters, and there writes his own.
> 'Here none approach,' said he, 'to interfere,
> But I can think of my Cecilia here.'

At length someone does approach; but the intrusion is not alarming:

> But there did come—and how it came to pass
> Who shall explain?—a mild and blue-eyed lass;—
> It was the work of accident, no doubt—
> The cause unknown—we say, 'as things fall out;'
> The damsel enter'd there, in wand'ring round about:
> At first she saw not Henry; and she ran,
> As from a ghost, when she beheld a man.

She is, Crabbe tells us, an orphan, niece to the steward and his wife. The 'grave old couple' keep Fanny secluded 'from every hero's sight'; but she cannot be kept literally locked up, and the timid girl wanders through unfrequented parts of the mansion

> looking, as she glides,
> On pictures, busts, and what she met besides,
> And speaking softly to herself alone,
> Or singing low in melancholy tone.

It is on one of these rambles that she happens to come upon Henry. On recovering from her fright, she contrives another 'chance' meeting. But there is surely no cause for anxiety, for

> of the meeting of a modest maid
> And sober youth why need we be afraid?
> And when a girl's amusements are so few
> As Fanny's were, what would you have her do?
> Reserved herself, a decent youth to find,
> And just be civil, sociable, and kind,
> And look together at the setting sun,
> Then at each other—what the evil done?

The answer is already hinted at as the question is posed. The remainder of the story is devoted to showing the emergence of the answer; and the narrative continues quietly, with an ironical ambiguity. First the demure Fanny

> took my little lord to play,
> And bade him not intrude on Henry's way:
> 'O, he intrudes not!' said the Youth, and grew
> Fond of the child. . . .

(The single word 'grew' lets us know that this diversion became habitual.) Then 'it chanced' that the pair met one night as they wandered in the park:

> Not in the common path, for so they might,
> Without a wonder, wander day or night;
> But, when in pathless ways their chance will bring
> A musing pair, we do admire the thing.

Henry and Fanny, for their part, admire the 'sweet light so brilliant on the stream' and the 'sweet music' of the cascade; and they also admire each other's sensibility towards nature. But Fanny declines an invitation to sit on a mossy seat, afraid (as she asserts with tears) not of Henry but of censorious tongues. And Henry, filled with 'emotions very warm and sweet', asks himself:

> 'What evil in discourse
> With one so guarded, who is pleased to trust
> Herself with me, reliance strong and just?'

By now the question does not strike the reader as merely rhetorical. But Henry decides that it would be unmanly to show coldness towards 'the maid who gave him her esteem', while as for Cecilia,

> It would be wrong in her to take amiss
> A virtuous friendship for a girl like this.

Besides, when the sun is absent,

> 'those starry twinklers may obtain
> A little worship till he shines again.'

Cecilia is displeased by Henry's overlong visit to his patron, even though he stays in deference to his father's wishes; but the tone of distant reproof in her letters only increases her lover's vanity. Henry and Fanny continue to meet daily

> as by consent,
> And yet it always seem'd by accident,

until Henry cannot fail to notice her affection for him. He resolves to fly, and does not fly. Fanny, meanwhile, awaits a declaration of love which he has no intention of making. Cecilia is still 'mistress of his mind'; yet she is absent, and the 'fondness' of the more demonstrative Fanny appeals to his vanity and becomes 'a present good, from which he dared not fly'. Indeed, his vanity so far blinds him that he even sings her praises in his letters to Cecilia.

Every morning he intends to end this 'dangerous friendship'; every night he is tormented by the thought that he has not carried out his 'prudent purpose'. He often wonders, too, why the dragon-aunt and uncle are so slack in keeping watch, but refuses to think that they have a design in their seeming negligence. He ignores his patron's kindly hint ('My good friend Harry, do not think us blind!'), but is pained when his father reminds him that, though love is a folly, 'something still is to our honour due'. Cecilia sends a far plainer warning—'You write too darkly, and you stay too long'—speaks of 'reports', and bids him 'instantly return'. The incensed Henry contrasts her haughtiness with Fanny's compliance; yet

> Uneasy, anxious, fill'd with self-reproof,
> He now resolved to quit his patron's roof;
> And then again his vacillating mind
> To stay resolved, and that her pride should find:
> Debating thus, his pen the lover took,
> And chose the words of anger and rebuke.

But even now he intends to confess the truth to Fanny, confident that

> 'by slow degrees
> She will regain her peace, and I my ease.'

So far the story has been an aggregation of details which take only a few lines each to record—very brief scenes, swift descriptions, fragments of letters, of soliloquies and of conversations. Not a single one is at all striking in itself; not one appears to mark a decisive step forward, much less to herald a crisis. Collectively, however, they amount to a good deal, and the action, which appears to mark time, is continuously advancing. Even without having the way charted for us by the tart, sardonic moralising which Crabbe intersperses here and there, we should be able to see that Henry, who thinks egress a simple matter to manage, has wandered very near to the centre of the maze.

But soon a day that was their doubts to close,
On the fond maid and thoughtless youth arose.

For in the heart of the maze Fanny's genially implacable guardians are waiting for Henry. Now comes the only prolonged 'scene' in the tale. As in *Resentment*, the crucial phase is rendered almost wholly in dialogue. But in *this* scene the principal character is in no way in control of events; Henry appears rather as the quarry who has been successfully ambushed, and whose fate now comes upon him suddenly and ineluctably.

Henry and Fanny, on their usual ramble in the park, meet Johnson the steward. This is the first time we have seen him at close quarters, and his sober, solid appearance proclaims him to be a person of consequence—accustomed, too, to having his own way. In a tone of friendly condescension, he at once begins to speak reassuringly of Fanny's dowry. The terrified Henry fails to stem the flow of ponderously arch congratulation, and the steward, going off without the youth's explanation, hands him over to the aunt, who 'happens' to hurry along at that moment. She has a sentimental coyness which is no improvement on her husband's manner; she is equally loquacious and equally firm in her assumption that all the young couple want is the blessing of their elders. With sinister unction, she assures him that this will be forthcoming. She favours him with a short sketch of his courtship of Fanny from a fresh angle:

'Think you, you walk'd unseen? There are who bring
To me all secrets—O, you wicked thing!'

She recounts Fanny's blushing confidences, and—worse still—tells him of the 'plot' contrived by herself and her husband to further the match, in concert with the earl and countess ('she's a lover's friend'). Again, the young man is scarcely allowed a moment's utterance. The aunt insists that she has no more time to spare, but she hands him his letters with a most ominous garrulity:

> 'Here are your letters—that's a female pen,
> Said I to Fanny—"'Tis his sister's, then,"
> Replied the maid.—No! never must you stray;
> Or hide your wanderings, if you should, I pray . . .
> I prattle idly, while your letters wait . . .
>   . . . do clear that clouded face,
> And with good looks your lucky lot embrace.
>   'Now, mind that none with her divide your heart,
> For she would die ere lose the smallest part;
> And I rejoice that all has gone so well,
> For who th'effect of Johnson's rage can tell?
> He had his fears when you began to meet,
> But I assured him there was no deceit:
> He is a man who kindness will requite,
> But, injured once, revenge is his delight.'

Henry is prevented from reflecting on either the ironical or the threatening aspect of this speech by the contents of Cecilia's letter. Scandal, she says, has informed her that he pursues a servant girl whose birth and virtue are highly dubious. Her angry ultimatum (he is to return within a day or else stay where he is and 'be with slaves a slave') fills him with defiance and thoughts of revenge. The timid Fanny appearing at that instant, Henry proposes, and ' "I will", she softly whisper'd.'

Nothing remains now but to round off the story. What Crabbe gives us is much unlike the powerful abruptness with which *Resentment* ends. Henry's bonds have to be firmly and lawfully knotted; and this is done in a lingering way. Crabbe has, in fact, told his story in a terse style (even the loquacity of the Johnsons, dramatically necessary, has been skilfully compressed), but he has appeared to be in no hurry. And now, before tying up the loose ends, he gives us an elaborate picture of Henry looking at the landscape on the following morning. The nature of the story permits this. It is the first (and last) minute description of external nature that we are given, but it is not an excrescence. It provides a short breathing-space after the tension of the proposal scene, and also—for it is a 'psychological landscape'—serves as an emblem of Henry's future:

> Early he rose, and look'd with many a sigh
> On the red light that fill'd the eastern sky;
> Oft had he stood before, alert and gay,
> To hail the glories of the new-born day:
> But now dejected, languid, listless, low,
> He saw the wind upon the water blow,
> And the cold stream curl'd onward as the gale
> From the pine-hill blew harshly down the dale;
> On the right side the youth a wood survey'd
> With all its dark intensity of shade;
> Where the rough wind alone was heard to move,
> In this, the pause of nature and of love,
> When now the young are rear'd, and when the old,
> Lost to the tie, grow negligent and cold—
> Far to the left he saw the huts of men,
> Half hid in mist, that hung upon the fen;
> Before him swallows, gathering for the sea,
> Took their short flights, and twitter'd on the lea;
> And near the bean-sheaf stood, the harvest done,
> And slowly blacken'd in the sickly sun;
> All these were sad in nature, or they took
> Sadness from him, the likeness of his look,
> And of his mind—he ponder'd for a while,
> Then met his Fanny with a borrow'd smile.[1]

[1] For further comment on this passage (ll. 701-24), see below, pp. 141-2.

The epilogue is short. The necessary arrangements for Henry's unintended marriage are easily completed; Cecilia's guardians are silent from scorn, and she herself

> seem'd as one who from a dream awoke;
> So all was peace, and soon the married pair
> Fix'd with fair fortune in a mansion fair.

The action then jumps forward five years, so that we may have a brief (but comprehensive) view of the expected retribution. All is thoroughly in character. Henry is

> The most repining of repenting men;
> With a fond, teasing, anxious wife, afraid
> Of all attention to another paid;
> Yet powerless she her husband to amuse,
> Lives but t' entreat, implore, resent, accuse;
> Jealous and tender, conscious of defects,
> She merits little, and yet much expects;
> She looks for love that now she cannot see,
> And sighs for joys that never more can be;
> On his retirements her complaints intrude,
> And fond reproof endears his solitude:
> While he her weakness (once her kindness) sees,
> And his affections in her languor freeze;
> Regret, uncheck'd by hope, devours his mind,
> He feels unhappy, and he grows unkind.

The process which we followed up to its climax in the proposal scene is continuing as it would be bound to continue; and the wealth of significant detail in the earlier part of the story illumines the closely-packed passage just quoted. As a gloomy pendant to his earlier soliloquies, Henry is allowed one more passage of reflection, this time a lament for his folly in abandoning 'the glory of her sex' to become 'an idiot's slave' for whom the future can bring nothing but

> Th' eternal clicking of the galling chains.

And the final incident in the tale—an inadvertent encounter with Cecilia, who faces him 'with brow severe' —testifies to the accuracy with which he has described his plight.

V

THE PICTORIAL ELEMENT

'THE adept in Dutch interiors, hovels and pig-styes,' says Hazlitt, 'must find in Mr. Crabbe a man after his own heart. He is the very thing itself; he paints in words instead of colours: there is no other difference.' Crabbe's contemporaries were impressed by his particularised rendering of the visible world. Jeffrey and Hazlitt both emphasise the affinity between his descriptive passages and paintings—Jeffrey, like Hazlitt, refers specifically to Dutch painting, but he also finds a 'Chinese accuracy' in *The Parish Register*. The poet himself often speaks of his work in terms appropriate to painting. In this, however, he is not necessarily doing more than complying with an eighteenth-century fashion. And Hazlitt's epigram—'he paints in words instead of colours'—is palpably no more than a suggestive metaphor.

How much Crabbe knew or cared about painting, and about the picturesque in landscape, is uncertain. According to his son, he was remarkably indifferent to painting and to 'what a painter's eye considers the beauties of landscape'. That this is an exaggeration is clear from Crabbe's poetry. The '*beauties* of landscape' certainly do not appear prominently in his work, but they are to be found; and there are many passages which reveal an appreciation of the *picturesque* in the visible world. As for his response to painting, there is a passage of about eighty lines in the largely autobio-

graphical tale, *The Happy Day* (*Posthumous Tales*, I),
describing the pictures which a little boy sees at Silford
Hall, and written in a manner suggesting that the
author derived some pleasure from looking at pictures;
he had, at least, learnt to comment on Dutch and
Flemish painting, and on Claude, in a 'correct', if perfunctory, way.[1] He can scarcely have avoided picking
up a little knowledge of painting when he was a young
man in London. In 1783, his son tells us, he 'very frequently passed his mornings at the easel of Sir Joshua
Reynolds, conversing on a variety of subjects, while this
distinguished artist was employed upon that celebrated
painting, the Infant Hercules, then preparing for the
Empress of Russia'.[2] Crabbe, to judge by the passage
in *The Happy Day*, appreciated Reynolds's skill in
rendering the expression of the human face on canvas;
but it has to be admitted that the only remark on painting made by the distinguished artist which the poet is
known to have remembered was by no means of an
aesthetic nature—namely, 'that this was his fourth
painting on the same canvas'.

Nor is there any evidence that he was at all closely
acquainted with current theories concerning the relation between poetry and painting.[3] His occasional
statements on the subject are not particularly illuminat-
ing. His awareness of an affinity between the two arts is

[1] His comments are of a kind which might have been derived from a
reading of Uvedale Price's *Dialogue on the Picturesque*.

[2] *Life*, p. 122.

[3] What knowledge he had is more likely to have been gained from
Reynolds's *Discourses* and Du Fresnoy's *De Arte Graphica* than from
Lessing's *Laocoön*. (Mason's verse translation of Du Fresnoy had been
annotated by Reynolds; the prose translation with preface, by Dryden,
was also widely read in the eighteenth century.)

borne out by his complaint, in the preface to the *Tales*, of the injustice of those critics who applaud accuracy of representation in painting while withholding the name of poetry from 'verses which strongly and faithfully delineate character and manners'. In *The Borough*, on the other hand, he has something to say about the different spheres in which the two arts can best succeed:

> Cities and towns, the various haunts of men,
> Require the pencil; they defy the pen; . . .
> Of Sea or River, of a Quay or Street,
> The best description must be incomplete;
> But when a happier theme succeeds, and when
> Men are our subjects and the deeds of men;
> Then may we find the Muse in happier style.[1]

He thus allows painting supremacy in representing the inanimate part of the visible world, and poetry supremacy in representing human subjects. He appears to have thought that, ideally, the description of a scene would record the *whole* truth, and in his own descriptions of the visible world he evidently accepted the incompleteness of the performance as a limitation imposed by his art of words. (In representing 'men and the deeds of men' he is always—designedly—selective.) It is true that in many of his descriptive passages he apparently *tries* to give verbal equivalents of pictures, as far as this can be done.[2] Still, accurate delineation is not

---

[1] Letter I; *Works*, III, pp. 17, 29-30; ll. 7-8, 297-301.

[2] It was not only Hazlitt who accepted them as verbal equivalents of pictures. Jeffrey calls *The Parish Register* a 'series of portraits . . . drawn with inimitable accuracy and strength of colouring'. In his review of *The Borough* he is explicit in comparing descriptive poetry with 'the kindred art of painting'; and in the course of rebuking Crabbe for wasting his graphic powers on unworthy objects he writes of the description

identical with complete transcription; and what Crabbe chiefly aimed at—actuality of relation, especially in dealing with character and manners—is something different from either.

His practice is superior to his theory. It is certain that he was well aware empirically of what each art could do best, and that he learnt the limitations and potentialities of descriptive poetry at an early date. The famous description of the Suffolk landscape in *The Village* reveals a keen perception of how far a scene may or should be rendered in words. The poet does not here attempt to effect with words something analogous to what the artist achieves with paint and canvas; and yet he adopts a manner which more than once suggests to the reader paint, canvas and the principles of the picturesque. We are promised a true picture of the 'frowning coast' where the writer had the misfortune to be born. Crabbe points out the irrelevance of conventional pastoral poetry to the actual poor, for whom 'the smoothest song is smooth in vain':

> Can poets soothe you, when you pine for bread,
> By winding myrtles round your ruin'd shed?

Having thus prepared us, by this opposition between *poetic* art and actual country life, for the antithesis between *pictorial* art and rural actuality which he is going to use, he proceeds to describe a field in which the rye which is to make the bread is struggling to grow:

of the 'vast old boarded room or warehouse' which was let out to beggars and vagabonds (Letter XVIII): 'No Dutch painter ever presented an interior more distinctly to the eye; or ever gave half such a group to the imagination' (*op. cit.* p. 327).

Lo! where the heath, with withering brake grown o'er,
Lends the light turf that warms the neighbouring poor;
From thence a length of burning sand appears,
Where the thin harvest waves its wither'd ears;
Rank weeds, that every art and care defy,
Reign o'er the land, and rob the blighted rye:
There thistles stretch their prickly arms afar,
And to the ragged infant threaten war;
There poppies nodding, mock the hope of toil;
There the blue bugloss paints the sterile soil;
Hardy and high, above the slender sheaf,
The slimy mallow waves her silky leaf;
O'er the young shoot the charlock throws a shade,
And clasping tares cling round the sickly blade;
With mingled tints the rocky coasts abound,
And a sad splendour vainly shines around.[1]

The first four lines mark out the area of the picture—
an expanse of heath and an adjacent expanse of sand—
but they do more than this. The importance of the soil
to those who live on it is already insisted on in 'the light
turf that warms the neighbouring poor' and clearly implied again in the 'wither'd ears' of the 'thin harvest'.
The next couplet, introducing the weeds, explains the
'thin harvest'. The picturesque is now abandoned, and
the victorious struggle of weeds against men is insisted
on ('defy . . . reign . . . rob'). The catalogue of weeds
which follows is, socially and economically, the most
important part of the scene. In it the attribution of
hostile intent to the weeds (a transparent but appropriate
fancy) is at first maintained—the thistles stretching
their arms threateningly, the poppies mocking the hope
of toil—and then the picturesque makes a sinister reappearance as 'the blue bugloss paints the sterile soil'.

[1] *Works*, II, p. 77; ll. 63-78.

The weeds, more strikingly in evidence than the blades
of rye, are differentiated with a necessary minimum of
detail—not enough to enable the reader to visualise
them, nor enough to enable him to identify them in
actuality if he does not know them already, but enough
to provide each with *some* character. The effect of this
part of the passage is not to sketch a picture. Strictly
visual detail is, in fact, extremely meagre; we hear more
about what the plants are like to the touch ('prickly . . .
slimy . . . silky'), and still more about their activities.
When the charlock throws a shade over the young shoot
this is not merely a dark patch in a picture; what is
more important is that the shoot is deprived of the light
it needs for growth. Accurate information is here conveyed in terms intelligible to those who are not botanists.
But Crabbe knows when to bring his list to an end: he
needs to name particular weeds, and to name enough
varieties to make it clear that the corn is bound to be
smothered, but he has also to avoid a tedious excess of
detail. The mallow, with its four adjectives and its
triumphant verb, receives a good deal of attention, after
which Crabbe becomes less copious over the charlock,
while the 'clasping tares' (unspecified) prepare us for
the end-couplet in which only the typical features of the
scene (now viewed from a distance) are pointed out.
We have the generalised 'rocky coasts', correctly
picturesque in their 'mingled tints', and the characteristic tone or mood of the scene—'sad splendour'—
is indicated. But the word 'vainly' serves to remind us
that the picturesqueness of the scene is lost on the inhabitants, who have no leisure or taste for it.

Thus we begin and end with the picturesque and
the general, and are given a hinted reminder of the

picturesque in the middle of the passage by the word 'paints'. Conversely, the question of the utility of the land to human beings is not lost sight of in the 'picturesque' couplets, and it is the justification (not merely the pretext) for the account of the weeds which occupies most of the passage. The function of the passage as a whole is to demonstrate that if you look closely enough into a picturesque landscape you are led, by way of agricultural problems, to consider the welfare of human beings. It will be found that most of Crabbe's descriptive passages of any length do something else as well as describe; I shall return to this topic later.

In considering the pictorial element in the work of any poet two facts have to be borne in mind. The first is that it is impossible to render in words simultaneously a scene which can be viewed *as a whole*, either in actuality or on canvas, in a single moment.[1] The second is that the poet can decide the order in which the component parts of the scene can be brought to the reader's notice.

It is said that the poet, in rendering a scene, is sometimes able by artifice to create an illusion of simultaneity. I do not think that Crabbe can often be said to do this, nor does he appear to have striven to do so.[2] He comes nearest to it in passages which convey an im-

[1] Dryden had an interesting afterthought on this subject: 'The Action, the Passion, and the Manners of so many Persons as are contain'd in a *Picture*, are to be discern'd at once, in the twinkling of an Eye; at least they would be so, if the Sight could travel over so many different Objects all at once, or the Mind could digest them all at the same Instant, or point of Time' (preface to his translation of Du Fresnoy's *De Arte Graphica*, ed. of 1716, pp. xxvi-xxvii).

[2] His longer descriptions are accounts of the component parts of a scene. Of the description of the group of gipsies in *The Lover's Journey* Jeffrey remarks that it is a picture which is 'evidently finished *con amore*'. It is certainly finished *con amore*, but it is not a pictorial group.

pression of a scene in three or four lines; and these are often parts of narrative sequences. *The Borough* provides many examples. Sometimes the scene is almost wholly conventional:

> Rich is that varied view with woods around,
> Seen from the seat, within the shrubb'ry bound;
> Where shines the distant lake, and where appear
> From ruins bolting, unmolested deer.[1]

(Here only the word 'bolting' suggests first-hand observation, and that preference for the particular rather than the general which is characteristic of Crabbe's descriptions.) Much more typical are these lines from *Peter Grimes*:

> When tides were neap, and, in the sultry day,
> Through the tall bounding mud-banks made their way,
> Which on each side rose swelling, and below
> The dark warm flood ran silently and slow;

or this fragment from the felon's dream in the twenty-third Letter:

> Then through the broomy bound with ease they pass,
> And press the sandy sheep-walk's slender grass,
> Where dwarfish flowers among the gorse are spread,
> And the lamb browses by the linnet's bed.

Both these passages, however, are only parts of comparatively elaborate narrative-descriptive sequences. Crabbe seems to find description scarcely worth doing unless it is fairly particularised. He will sometimes begin with a series of swiftly sketched contrasts, as in some lines on the sea in the first Letter of *The Borough*:

> Its colours changing, when from clouds and sun
> Shades after shades upon the surface run;

[1] Letter I; *Works*, III, p. 21.

> Embrown'd and horrid now, and now serene,
> In limpid blue, and evanescent green;
> And oft the foggy banks on ocean lie,
> Lift the fair sail, and cheat th' experienc'd eye.[1]

But this is followed by far more minute companion-pictures, one of the sea at noon in summer, the other of a winter storm, both rich in carefully observed and meticulously recorded detail:

> Ships in the calm seem anchor'd; for they glide
> On the still sea, urg'd solely by the tide.

It will be seen that Crabbe is no less aware of change and movement in the visible world than of the incessant changes in human beings; much of his description, therefore, is narrative, strictly speaking. Sometimes he contrives to convey an impression of a continually changing scene so swiftly that he may be said to achieve the paradox of suggesting continuous movement in a momentary glimpse of the scene:

> The moon was risen, and she sometimes shone
> Through thick white clouds, that flew tumultuous on,
> Passing beneath her with an eagle's speed,
> That her soft light imprison'd and then freed.[2]

Occasionally the poet succeeds in depicting a composite but unified scene in such a way that the whole may be imagined as present to the eye. One of the most

[1] He adds a wholly characteristic note: 'Of the effect of these mists, known by the name of fog-banks, wonderful and, indeed, incredible relations are given; but their property of appearing to elevate ships at sea, and to bring them in view is, I believe, generally acknowledged'.

[2] *Smugglers and Poachers* (*Tales of the Hall*, XXI); *Works*, VII, p. 271. Crabbe follows this with a comment (which is rare for him) on the beauty of the scene. This may be regarded as a touch of pictorial irony: the woman making her way by the light of the moon has no eyes for the scene, only ears for the menacingly 'roaring winds and rushing waters'; she is shortly to come upon the dead bodies of her husband and lover.

striking passages of this kind, a unit complete in itself, is the description, in *Villars*, of the surroundings of the 'large old mansion, suffer'd to decay':

> Dark elms around the constant herons bred,
> Those the marsh dykes, the neighbouring ocean, fed;
> Rocks near the coast no shipping would allow,
> And stubborn heath around forbad the plough;
> Dull must the scene have been in years of old,
> But now was wildly dismal to behold—
> One level sadness! marsh, and heath, and sea,
> And, save those high dark elms, nor plant nor tree.

Here the component elements in the scene are brought before us in swift succession in lines remarkable for their compact informativeness (Crabbe has, indeed, sacrificed elegance to compactness in the third line); then the character of the scene is pointed, both in its physical and in its emotional aspect ('one level sadness'); after which the parts are again named, the concluding couplet thus summing up the whole scene.

Generally, however, Crabbe's descriptions might more appropriately be termed cinematographic than pictorial. He turns to advantage in various ways the poet's power to determine the order in which the different parts of a scene are to be presented to the reader. Sometimes the order of presentation conveys knowledge of, and implies a judgment on, some facet of human nature. The lines on Catherine Lloyd (*The Parish Register: Burials*) illustrate this clearly. Crabbe's task is comparatively simple; he has to give us a portrait of the lady, alluding obliquely to those incidents in her life-story which he needs to fill out the portrait and render it intelligible. He shows us what she was like mainly by describing her house and its contents—and her attitude to its contents. Towards the end of the sketch Crabbe becomes quite explicit about her attitude, but he has previously used his peculiar art of portraiture to make clear the salient fact about her character: that avarice has killed every other feeling in her. He achieves this by the simple method of enumerating the contents of her parlour in the order in which they are valued by Catherine Lloyd—with the not insignificant exception of the love-letters, which are placed among the treasures having a high cash value. The resulting passage[1] can scarcely be called a description of a room, for, while the details are precise, no picture of the whole is conveyed —nor is it necessary for Crabbe's purpose that it should be.

First come the 'long-priz'd treasures' given her by a Captain 'rich from India', on whose account

> evil fame—(but that was long before)
> Had blown her dubious blast at *Catherine*'s door.

She has

> Silks beyond price, so rich, they'd stand alone,
> And diamonds blazing on the buckled zone;
> Rows of rare pearls by curious workmen set,
> And bracelets fair in box of glossy jet. . . .

and, among various other treasures (the list is rather long):

> Letters, long proofs of love, and verses fine
> Round the pink'd rims of crisped Valentine.

Mere paper (however fine the workmanship of the Valentines) comes a little oddly among the diamonds and pearls. The letters are, so to speak, the fossilised remains of their owner's youth, no longer possessing

[1] *Works*, II, pp. 212-13; ll. 326-71.

even a sentimental value. For Catherine is 'in maiden-state immured'; her china-closet with its

> pictured wealth of China and Japan,
> Like its cold mistress, shunn'd the eye of man.

These are the treasures on which her heart is set. Still, she is not wholly devoid of feeling for the animate. Next in order come her pets: a clipped French puppy, a parrot (which is, however, 'dead and stuff'd with art' as a result of its unlucky habit of swearing), an old grey cat ('A type of sadness in the house of pride') and two fish, one gold and one silver, in an ivory-framed globe:

> All these were form'd the guiding taste to suit;
> The beasts well-manner'd and the fishes mute.

And last of all, the only other human occupant comes in for a brief mention:

> A widow'd Aunt was there, compell'd by need
> The nymph to flatter and her tribe to feed;
> Who, veiling well her scorn, endured the clog,
> Mute as the fish and fawning as the dog.

The detail is copious. But it is not true that Crabbe habitually describes everything that is there, as Hazlitt suggests. Hazlitt, irritated by Crabbe's citing Pope's lines on the Duke of Buckingham 'as a parallel instance of merely literal description' in a defence of his own manner of writing, asserts that nothing can be more dissimilar than the methods of these two poets, and that Pope, by describing what is striking, is able to show what is passing 'in a poetical light'. In the critic's view, Crabbe's peculiarity lay in the microscopic, and hence all-inclusive, nature of his descriptions; since they lacked contrast, there was 'no impulse given to the mind'. No one would deny that Crabbe's descriptions make a less striking use of contrast than Pope's. But it is clear that Crabbe's method is not microscopic but selective; and the passage on Catherine Lloyd employs gradation as its principle of organisation.

The successful use of descriptive passages in short narrative poems demands a somewhat different skill and presents more complex problems than Crabbe had to face in the sketch of Catherine Lloyd, or in the description of the field of rye in *The Village*. His tales contain many highly finished descriptions; but these, in order to be acceptable as parts of a composite whole, must have psychological value and relevance to the narrative itself.

The description of the farmer's family and servants at dinner, in the opening lines of *The Widow's Tale* (*Tales*, VII), is, as Jeffrey observed, 'in Mr. Crabbe's best style of Dutch painting'. The composition has its human element—the farmer laying a pound of beef at once on his plate, his son 'hot from the field', and the men, maids and cook beside them—and its element of still life, the huge wooden bowl

> Fill'd with huge balls of farinaceous food;
> With bacon, mass saline, where never lean
> Beneath the brown and bristly rind was seen;

and the horn from which they all drink 'copious draughts of heavy ale and new'. Jeffrey's objection, that this is 'a little coarse and needlessly minute', shows a failure to perceive the function of the passage or to discern how a descriptive passage of this kind differs from painting. The description is prefaced by a brief sketch of the farmer's daughter, just back from school, where she has acquired 'pretty talents' and an excess of fastidiousness, so that she is scarcely able to endure the meal in her father's kitchen:

> The swelling fat in lumps conglomerate laid,
> And fancy's sickness seized the loathing maid.

The reason for Crabbe's insistence, in the lines that follow these, on the abundance and fatty solidity of the food and on the uncouth manners of the 'rude hinds who cut and came again' is, clearly, that these things lacerate the pampered sensibility of the girl whose fortunes he is to record. She herself comes prominently into the picture at the end of the passage:

> She could not breathe; but with a heavy sigh,
> Rein'd the fair neck, and shut th' offended eye;
> She minced the sanguine flesh in frustums fine,
> And wonder'd much to see the creatures dine.

But she makes more than one appearance. She has been referred to twice earlier in the passage, so that we are prepared to accept the lines as not only an account of a scene but also an account of the impact which this scene makes on her. And her reappearance at the end of the description leads us back to the narrative proper: the story of her reorientation.

The autumnal landscape in *Delay has Danger* (quoted above, page 125), similarly, has more than a purely descriptive function. This passage, I suggested earlier, serves two purposes in the narrative structure: it provides relaxation after the tension of the scene in which Henry is interviewed by the steward and his wife and proposes to Fanny, and it also serves as a kind of emblematic epilogue. This dual function accounts for its length, its minuteness and its arrangement. Its opening announces a scene viewed by a man in dejection, and the landscape—in sound and temperature as well as in its purely visual elements—matches the mood. The observer seeks a short respite from action; and the details of the landscape are given as they would present themselves to someone allowing his eye to wander over a large tract of country, not all of which could be focused simultaneously. A correspondence between human and non-human life is pointed by the poet (in autumn there comes 'the pause of nature and of love'), but the human element in the scene itself amounts to no more than what is suggested by the distant huts on the fen, half-hidden by mist. From surveying these, the observer's eye passes to the less distant swallows; and after this the most obviously unpleasing detail, the decaying bean-sheaf that 'slowly blacken'd in the sickly sun', is attached like a leaden pendant to the end of the list. Finally, the correspondence and interaction between the observed and the observer is re-emphasised:

> All these were sad in nature, or they took
> Sadness from him, the likeness of his look,
> And of his mind.

One other pictorial passage needs to be noticed—the description of the 'boundless plain' in *Sir Eustace Grey*. It resembles the passage just discussed solely in being a landscape that is presented as it strikes a beholder who is a character in the poem. The lines from *Sir Eustace Grey* give what is literally a psychological landscape: Sir Eustace, a victim of agonising hallucinations, is telling the story of his supposed adventures to a visitor to the madhouse where he is confined; he recounts how, as a punishment for his sins, he became the prey of 'two fiends of darkness' who would allow him no repose:

Through lands we fled, o'er seas we flew,
　　And halted on a boundless plain;
Where nothing fed, nor breathed, nor grew,
　　But silence ruled the still domain.

Upon that boundless plain, below,
　　The setting sun's last rays were shed,
And gave a mild and sober glow,
　　Where all were still, asleep, or dead;
Vast ruins in the midst were spread,
　　Pillars and pediments sublime,
Where the grey moss had form'd a bed,
　　And clothed the crumbling spoils of time.

There I was fix'd, I know not how,
　　Condemn'd for untold years to stay:
Yet years were not;—one dreadful *Now*
　　Endured no change of night or day;
The same mild evening's sleeping ray
　　Shone softly solemn and serene,
And all that time I gazed away,
　　The setting sun's sad rays were seen.[1]

Here is rendered a scene of mild, sad stillness, the peculiar horror of which, when it is at length revealed, is found to lie precisely in its complete immobility. The stillness, as well as the vastness, of the plain where Sir Eustace is halted after rapid flight is insisted on from the start. But the second stanza displays a landscape which, if desolate, is not yet terrifying: it is a *sublime* landscape in Burke's sense of the word. Sir Eustace observes the 'mild and sober glow' of the setting sun's last rays, and the ruins have the remote grandeur of antiquity. By combining in a single scene the slowly mouldering ruins and the setting sun, which are

[1] *Works*, II, p. 269; ll. 192-211.

pictorially harmonious, Crabbe makes us aware at the same time of the lapse of centuries and the lapse of a day. In all this there is nothing that could not be either represented or suggested by a painter. But the poet, because he is working in the medium of words, is able to round off his scene with a phrase which brings the idea of time into his reader's mind: 'the crumbling spoils of time' suggests the very slow decomposition of a very durable substance.

But still, this second stanza, carefully preparing the way for the third, has nothing that is palpably menacing. In the wholly unpaintable third stanza, Sir Eustace's torment consists in the discovery that he is (or so he thinks) doomed to be a perpetual spectator of the unchanging. Retaining a consciousness of the passage of time in his own mind ('all that time I gazed away'), he confronts what seems to be an actual landscape possessing the timelessness of a painting—a timelessness visibly marked by the position of the sun, always tantalisingly on the horizon. And it is the 'softly solemn' *serenity* of the visible scene, at once inviting and preventing sleep, that paradoxically contributes most to the agony of the observer.

VI

WHY NOT IN PROSE?

'WHY not insist on the unwelcome reality in plain prose?' This question was posed by Hazlitt in *The Spirit of the Age*; but Crabbe must have asked himself the same question long before. Just after the turn of the century he wrote three novels. The first had as its principal character a 'benevolent humourist'. The next, in a more sombre vein, was called *Reginald Glanshaw, or the Man who commanded Success*, and is described by the younger Crabbe as 'a portrait of an assuming, over-bearing, ambitious mind, rendered interesting by some generous virtues, and gradually wearing down into idiotism'. About the third novel the biographer records an instructive anecdote: 'I clearly remember that it opened with a description of a wretched room, similar to some that are presented in his poetry, and that, on my mother's telling him frankly that she thought the effect very inferior to that of the corresponding pieces in verse, he paused in his reading, and, after some reflection, said, "Your remark is just"'.[1] He proceeded to make a leisurely examination of his manuscript novels, and then burnt them and set to work on *The Parish Register*.

We have Crabbe's own word that he found himself unable to manage a complex plot in a verse tale; his awareness of this inability would sufficiently explain why he did not continue writing novels. Had he lived

---

[1] *Life*, p. 167.

a century later, he might well have written short stories; and yet the anecdote just related makes us doubt whether the short story would have been a happy choice of *genre* apart from its single advantage of allowing the author to confine himself to handling a simple plot. Evidently Crabbe was reading to his wife a *descriptive* passage forming the opening of the novel; and what Mrs. Crabbe and the poet himself perceived was that, for him, verse-writing led to better results because it involved a different way of using language from that of prose-writing. The son's comment—namely, that, judging by the simple elegance of language in Crabbe's prefaces and dedications, the novels would not have been defective in diction—quite misses the point that a very different style would have been desirable in a novel. Almost all Crabbe's extant prose is discursive: prefaces, sermons, writings on natural history and footnotes to his poems. The only exceptions, which give some slight indication of the probable style of his novels, are his letters and journals. These show, in varying degrees, the qualities of terseness and clarity, and they are enlivened with occasional touches of irony; but they have, also, a leisureliness, an evenness of texture, and a tendency towards the smooth convolutions of the periodic sentence, which suggest that the style of his prose fiction would have been wanting in variety and emphasis.

But apart from his lack of certain gifts requisite in the novelist, there are several reasons why Crabbe should have written in verse. To begin with, existing verse provided him with an abundance of precedents and models which were of great service to one whose traditionalism was, in part at least, caused by a want

of self-confidence, and even timidity. For the fittest
models in the verse tale he had to go back to Chaucer;
but in satire and in descriptive and didactic poetry, or
'moral essays', eighteenth-century writers served him
well. Almost every kind of writing that he could
confidently attempt, he must have felt, had been
practised before in one form or another. The social and
moral exhortation of *The Village*, the grave or satirical
character-sketches of *The Parish Register*, the descriptions, anecdotes and tales of *The Borough* (to say nothing
of the ostensible use of the familiar letter as a vehicle
for these matters)—for all these he had precedents.

Yet it was not only in matters of broad design, or in
the handling of a story or the layout of descriptions and
character sketches, that his models influenced him: they
affected him also in his peculiar mode of using language,
and in the habits of thought and feeling associated with
this kind of expression. It is with questions of diction, of
local texture, that the present chapter is chiefly concerned.

It was said of the euphonious Spenser that, having
the sound of ancient poets 'still ringing in his ears, he
must needs in singing hit out some of their tunes'.
Crabbe had the sounds of Dryden and Pope, of Johnson
and Goldsmith, ringing in his ears; but when he echoes
these sounds he can scarcely be said to give forth
archaic melodies. He grew up convinced that, to write
poetry in the correct way, he must keep within a certain
range of manner and diction, and that he would be able
to do this the more easily if, like his masters, he made
the heroic couplet his staple metre. Sometimes he
appears as no more than a competent disciple; and there
are many passages, in his earlier work especially, which

show proficiency in the neat, antithetical Augustan mode without achieving any marked distinction. The following lines from *The Parish Register*, describing pictures of naval battles, fairly represent the merely derivative strain in the poet:

> Now lo! on Egypt's coast that hostile fleet,
> By nations dreaded and by NELSON beat;
> And here shall soon another triumph come,
> A deed of glory in a day of gloom;
> Distressing glory! grievous boon of fate!
> The proudest conquest, at the dearest rate.

Occasionally he pays his masters the tribute of palpable imitation. This may take the form of respectful parody, as in the youthful *Inebriety*, where the poet (who apologises for having taken 'such great liberties with Mr. Pope') announces his theme with an unsophisticated aping of the opening lines of *The Dunciad*. More often the echoes betoken a different mood, the decorous following of a respected guide, as in this line from the elegiac passage in the second book of *The Village*:

> Oh! ever honour'd, ever valued! say—

which is patently based on Pope's

> Oh ever beauteous, ever friendly! tell.[1]

And, in a vein of sombre satire, Johnson's

> With weekly libels and septennial ale[2]

is easily transformed to

> The yearly dinner, or septennial bribe.[3]

Even though his versification has not Pope's sensitiveness of finish or Johnson's resonant strength or the soft

---

[1] *Elegy to the Memory of an Unfortunate Lady*, l. 5.
[2] *The Vanity of Human Wishes*, l. 97.
[3] *The Village*, Bk. I; *Works*, II, p. 78.

fluency of Goldsmith, Crabbe usually shows a sound enough sense of which is the best model to adopt in order to achieve some particular effect. Moreover, he learnt to borrow in an independent spirit. When we read his description of the Widow Goe nearing her end, with

> Heaven in her eye and in her hand her keys,

we may recall two progenitors of this line: Pope's frenzied poetasters in the *Epistle to Dr. Arbuthnot*:

> Fire in each eye, and papers in each hand,[1]

and Johnson's Cardinal Wolsey, with

> Law in his voice, and fortune in his hand.[2]

Crabbe's line has not (but does not need) the same degree of ludicrous particularisation that Pope achieves; nor has it the grave moral antithesis of Johnson's line, which is general and elevated. Instead, his critical vein takes the form of unambitious irony; moreover, his simple antithesis between this world and the next gains emphasis not only from the concreteness of the Widow's keys but also from the inversion which places them at the very end of the line.

An author, says Crabbe, ought not to use the words or ideas of another without acknowledgment. He prides himself on having avoided plagiarism in *The Borough*, but remarks: 'I do not affirm that much of sentiment and much of expression [in that work] may not be detected in the vast collection of English poetry'.[3] For, though plagiarism was a crime, it was laudable to try to discern the principles on which Pope or Johnson or Goldsmith (or, indeed, Chaucer) had written, and to

---

[1] Line 5. [2] *The Vanity of Human Wishes*, l. 100.
[3] *Works*, III, p. 38.

observe the same principles himself, so far as what he had to say allowed this.

The features of Crabbe's verse which are most closely related to the tradition of the age in which he was born are its ready intelligibility and its modes of achieving a concentration of meaning. Eighteenth-century standards in literary manners demanded of the poet, as of the prose-writer, that the sense of what he wrote should be capable of being understood by the average educated reader without mental wrestling. With this requirement Crabbe usually complies. His verse is seldom obscure; and when it is so, this is as a rule either because he has written carelessly or because his transitions are too abrupt.

That he possessed the power of concentration of meaning will perhaps less readily be allowed, if by 'concentration of meaning' we understand something distinct from what can be achieved in terse prose. Yet, although he was less generously endowed with this power than Pope, he had his share of it. It is revealed in several ways: firstly, in an inclination towards the aphoristic. Crabbe's aphorisms are marked by weight and pith rather than by brilliance. Because he cares more for truth than for wit, he gives us maxims or *sententiae* more often than epigrams. What he can do in this respect may be illustrated fairly by such a line as

Fertile is evil in the soul of man,[1]

or by this couplet:

Our feelings still upon our views attend,
And their own natures to the objects lend.[2]

[1] *The Parish Clerk* (*The Borough*, XIX); *Works*, III, p. 307.
[2] *The Lover's Journey* (*Tales*, X); *Works*, V, p. 21.

More often he tends towards the aphoristic without attaining the self-sufficient, detachable aphorism. He is a master (even if not a profuse one) of the pointed and penetrating phrase—'the cold charities of man to man', 'th' intenseness of the working thought', 'Laughing in languor, miserably gay'—and of the apt but *un*-arresting metaphor, as when he observes that time 'steals from virtue her asperities', or, of the poor man's over-numerous offspring, that 'They keep the sunshine of good humour out'.[1] Aphorisms are more sparse in the later poems than in the earlier, partly, no doubt, because by that time the poet gave less attention to the isolated verbal detail, but chiefly because the kind of narrative verse which he writes does not furnish many occasions for aphorisms. The epigrammatic line interrupts or impedes a narrative; more appropriate are expressions which vividly mark the end of a phase—

> melting into truth, the vision fled—

or briskly herald a new one:

> Twelve months her sables she in sorrow wore,
> And mourn'd so long that she could mourn no more,

or sum up the state of a character:

> Fix'd in her purpose, perfect in her part,
> She felt the courage of a wounded heart.[2]

All the lines quoted in this paragraph are perfectly clear in their sense; but in manner they are unlike the

---

[1] *The Village*, I; *Works*, II, p. 84: *The Mother* (*Tales*, VIII); *Works*, IV, p. 316: *The Elder Brother* (*Tales of the Hall*, VII); *Works*, VI, p. 153: *Arabella* (*Tales*, IX); *Works*, V, p. 12: *The Parish Register*, I (*Baptisms*); *Works*, II, p. 160.

[2] *The Natural Death of Love* (*Tales of the Hall*, XIV); *Works*, VII, p. 85: *The Frank Courtship* (*Tales*, VI); *Works*, IV, p. 268: *The Mother* (*Tales*, VIII); *Works*, IV, p. 314.

prose of the age, notably in the metaphorical use of verb and adjective and in the occasional oxymoron ('miserably gay'). The metre, too, exerts a moulding force; the classic couplet makes for swiftness and tautness, and the sense gains emphasis from the pattern imposed by rhyme and by the balancing of phrases within the line.

No less characteristic than the aphoristic strain are those forms of expression in which the full sense is taken only if we follow out the poet's implications as well as his statements. It is still true that anyone, reading rapidly, may follow the plain sense easily enough, but a more actively co-operative reader finds the plain sense enriched by overtones. Sometimes we may be required to recognise allusions to lines from other poets:

> His father early lost, his mother tried
> To live without him, liked it not, and—sigh'd,
> When, for her widow'd hand, an amorous youth applied.[1]

Readers who recognise the well-known epitaph echoed in the first two lines expect 'died' instead of 'sigh'd', so that the effect of the sequel is to combine a narrative detail with a faintly ironical comparison of the rare widow who died of grief with the more representative widow who was consoled. Similarly, our impression of Footman Daniel is modified by the recognition of a double allusion to Pope:

> And thus, with clouded cane, a fop complete,
> He stalk'd, the jest and glory of the street.[2]

Sir Plume, versed in 'the nice conduct of a clouded cane', was at least an authentically aristocratic fop and not a vulgar small-town imitation: and the insignifi-

[1] *The Brothers* (*Tales of the Hall*, II); *Works*, VI, p. 38.
[2] *The Parish Register*, II (*Marriages*); *Works*, II, p. 187.

cance of the sphere in which Daniel contrives to shine
is accentuated by the adaptation of the line:

> The glory, jest, and riddle of the world.[1]

Palpable allusion of this kind, however, is not very
common in Crabbe. More often than not, the implications which the reader has to perceive call into play, not
his memories of other poets, but his capacity for discrimination in matters of feeling and conduct, and more
particularly his sense of proportion, on which the inadequate or the excessive jars. The poet's implied in-
dictment of a character may take the form of ironical
defence or acquiescence: in one of the *Tales* of 1812 the
vain, unfeeling mother, who has prevented her daughter
from marrying an insufficiently eligible suitor, is aston-
ished when the girl obstinately pines away:

> Surprised, the Mother saw the languid frame,
> And felt indignant, yet forbore to blame:
> Once with a frown she cried, 'And do you mean
> To die of love—the folly of fifteen?'
> But as her anger met with no reply,
> She let the gentle girl in quiet die.[2]

It may be argued that similar effects are possible in
prose; this is true—but Crabbe achieves them more
crisply, economically and pointedly in verse.

Lines of the barest factual statement may also carry
implications which are immediately seen by the vigilant
reader and which are essential to the full understanding
of the passage. In *Procrastination*, when we are told of
Dinah:

> She knew that mothers grieved, and widows wept,
> And she was sorry, said her prayers, and slept,

[1] *The Rape of the Lock*, IV, 124. *An Essay on Man*, II, 18.
[2] *The Mother* (*Tales*, VIII); *Works*, IV, p. 314.

this brisk couplet alone would make us understand, without explicit statement, that Dinah has no longer any capacity for spontaneous feeling; her heart is as well regulated as the clock in her parlour which 'click'd from pray'r to pray'r, from meal to meal'. When no moral judgment is involved, Crabbe's descriptions may have a curious sardonic sobriety. In his sketch of the worthy Jonas Kindred there is both a relishing of Jonas's patriarchal gravity and a sense of its excessiveness—and hence of its absurdity. Jonas is a fine specimen of his type, but it is an unlovely type:

> Grave *Jonas Kindred*, Sybil Kindred's sire,
> Was six feet high, and looked six inches higher;
> Erect, morose, determined, solemn, slow,
> Who knew the man, could never cease to know;
> His faithful spouse, when Jonas was not by,
> Had a firm presence and a steady eye;
> But with her husband dropp'd her look and tone,
> And Jonas ruled unquestion'd and alone.[1]

On the surface, the manner is as staid and impassive as Jonas himself, but the seeming inconsequentiality of the second line sets flowing an undercurrent of irreverence.

Were it not so, there would be little in the passage, apart from 'who' for 'anyone who', and 'spouse', to distinguish it from Crabbe's neutral manner—a manner not maintained in its purity for long at a stretch, but continually returned to. By 'neutral manner' is meant an uncoloured, not an insipid, manner. Aphorism and implication may be absent, and the metaphorical strain may be as quiet as that of prose or common discourse, and yet a passage in the neutral manner may be unprosaic and, moreover, easily recognisable as Crabbe's

---

[1] The opening lines of *The Frank Courtship* (*Tales*, VI).

work. The mere fact of the poet's using a vocabulary which would serve equally well for prose does not lead to the neutral style. On the contrary, it is clear that every word in a sentence, considered in isolation, may be a 'prose' word, while the *collocation* of words is totally unprosaic. In *The Village*, for instance, describing the pauper's funeral, Crabbe writes:

And the glad parish pays the frugal fee—

a line consisting wholly of words appropriate to prose or common speech, but unprosaic in such collocations as 'glad parish' and 'frugal fee', which in non-poetic writing would appear as liberties taken with common usage, but which, in this context, combine perfect intelligibility with an unprosaic mode of concentration of meaning: 'the *glad* parish *pays*' excites our surprise after what we have been told of the parish officials, but '*frugal* fee' explains all, and it is unnecessary for the poet to dwell further on the triumph of avarice over humane feeling.

The simpler aspect of the uncoloured style in Crabbe is fairly shown in such passages as this fragment of the description of Jonas Kindred's house:

Neat was their house; each table, chair, and stool,
Stood in its place, or moving moved by rule;
No lively print or picture graced the room;
A plain brown paper lent its decent gloom.

Perhaps a neutral style might be expected especially in passages where Crabbe describes commonplace objects. But it is found equally in dialogue and narrative. The following lines form part of the account of Dinah's rejection of Rupert in *Procrastination*:

Here Dinah sigh'd, as if afraid to speak—
And then repeated—'They were frail and weak;

His soul she lov'd, and hoped he had the grace
To fix his thoughts upon a better place.'
She ceased;—with steady glance, as if to see
The very root of this hypocrisy,—
He her small fingers moulded in his hard
And bronzed broad hand; then told her his regard,
His best respect were gone, but love had still
Hold on his heart, and govern'd yet the will—
Or he would curse her:—saying this he threw
The hand in scorn away, and bade adieu
To every lingering hope, with every care in view.[1]

It may be remarked that here, while the vocabulary is
that of common discourse, and while the alterations in
the normal word-order are few and (since we are used
to such inversions in verse) do not obtrude themselves
on our notice as we read, Crabbe has nevertheless contrived to make the movement of his verse—the abrupt
pauses within the fifth and eleventh lines, the running-
over from the fifth to the sixth line and from the
seventh to the eighth—correspond to the irregular
movements of passion, manifested in expression and
vehement gesture, which he seeks to render.

The conclusion of *The Mother*, too, exemplifies his
plain style well. The mother, apparently undistressed by
her daughter's death, reverts to her main preoccupation
—her own beauty, to which she invites tributes:

Her picture then the greedy Dame displays;
Touch'd by no shame, she now demands its praise;
In her tall mirror then she shows a face,
Still coldly fair with unaffecting grace;
These she compares, 'It has the form,' she cries,
'But wants the air, the spirit, and the eyes;
This, as a likeness, is correct and true,
But there alone the living grace we view.'

[1] *Works*, IV, p. 228; ll. 287-99.

This said, th' applauding voice the Dame required,
And, gazing, slowly from the glass retired.

The cool informativeness of this passage contrasts with
the heightened tone of what has gone before, the
mother's lack of feeling being brought out the more
clearly by the uncoloured quality of the style. But to say
this is only to revert to the question of context discussed in an earlier chapter; and it might be added
that a contrast of this kind would be possible in a short
story in prose. What the metrical arrangement of
language contributes here is brevity of narration (a
prose writer would be likely to expand the statements
and indicate explicitly the relations between them); and,
further, the hard angularity and abruptness of rhythm
may be viewed as the metrical counterpart of that aspect
of the mother—her heart, not her appearance—which
Crabbe wants to leave us reflecting upon.

It will be observed that, while the terms which the
mother uses in her comparison of picture and reflection
are very much what would be expected of an amateur of
portrait-painting, her words have not a genuinely colloquial ring: the metre not only compels an uncol-
loquial conciseness but also emphasises the speaker's
antitheses. To adjust the language of common speech
to verse composition so that the tone of conversation is
suggested, but nevertheless to avoid ludicrous effects,
is a difficult task, especially when the metre used is one
associated principally with a manner either polished and
elegant or else (in satire sometimes) purposefully uncouth. Crabbe does not always solve the problem in the
same way. *The Natural Death of Love* (*Tales of the Hall*,
XIV), which Jeffrey praised as the 'best-written' in the
collection, is conceived as a *literary* dialogue, a debate in

verse, between a husband and wife typifying those for whom

> love dies away
> In gradual waste and unperceived decay,

and to whom their conversation brings a qualified acceptance of this 'natural death'. The character and attitude of each speaker are allowed to appear, and so are the changing feelings of each, as the debate takes its course. But the argument is tidier and more ceremonious than an actual argument; the ideas of both speakers are better marshalled, and are presented more eloquently and more rhetorically:

> *Emma*: Ah! much I doubt—when you in fury broke
> That lovely vase by one impassion'd stroke,
> And thousand china fragments met my sight,
> Till rising anger put my grief to flight;
> As well might you the beauteous jar repiece,
> As joy renew and bid vexation cease.
> *Henry*: Why then 'tis wisdom, Emma, not to keep
> These griefs in memory; they had better sleep.[1]

But when his purpose requires it, Crabbe can give a comparatively realistic rendering of a domestic quarrel, as he does in this passage from *The Mother*, in which a spoilt, petulant wife persists in *not* being pleased:

> Pleasure she sought, and, disappointed, sigh'd
> For joys, she said, 'to her alone denied;'
> And she was 'sure her parents, if alive,
> Would many comforts for their child contrive:'
> The gentle Husband bade her name him one;
> 'No—that,' she answer'd, 'should for her be done:
> How could she say what pleasures were around?
> But she was certain many might be found.'—

[1] *Works*, VII, p. 93; ll. 385-92.

'Would she some sea-port, Weymouth, Scarborough, grace?'
'He knew she hated every watering-place:'—
'The town?'—'What! now 'twas empty, joyless, dull?'
—'In winter?'—'No! she liked it worse when full.'
She talk'd of building—'Would she plan a room?'—
'No! she could live, as he desired, in gloom:'
'Call then our friends and neighbours:'—'He might call,
And they might come and fill his ugly hall;
A noisy vulgar set, he knew she scorn'd them all:'—
'Then might their two dear girls the time employ,
And their improvement yield a solid joy;'—
'Solid indeed! and heavy—oh! the bliss
Of teaching letters to a lisping miss!'—
'My dear, my gentle Dorothea, say,
Can I oblige you?'—'You may go away.'[1]

This has a fundamental realism of character; but as dialogue, too, it has a realistic basis. It is formalised bickering. The compromise between *oratio recta* and *oratio obliqua* removes it somewhat from the actual; and the wife's querulousness is made more pointed by the unnaturalistic compactness of Crabbe's expression, the necessary air of authenticity being still sufficiently maintained, as in

'. . . a solid joy;'—
'Solid indeed!'

The comparatively large scale of the tales permits greater realism of speech than is possible in the 'characters' of *The Parish Register*, which are, to some extent, *exempla*. Even here, it is true, actual-sounding speech may be appropriately used, and may be directly indicative of character, as are the words of Doctor

---

[1] *Works*, IV, pp. 306-7; ll. 39-61. This tale has also minor successes of the same nature:

[She] keenly felt the Mother's angry taunt,
'Thou art the image of thy pious Aunt.'

Grandspear, one of the five rectors described by the
sexton who has buried them:

> '*Ralph*,' would he say, '*Ralph Dibble*, thou art old;
> That doublet fit, 'twill keep thee from the cold:
> How does my sexton?—What! the times are hard;
> Drive that stout pig, and pen him in thy yard.'
> But most, his rev'rence loved a mirthful jest:—
> 'Thy coat is thin; why man, thou'rt *barely* dress'd;
> It's worn to th' thread; but I have nappy beer;
> Clap that within, and see how they will wear.'

But in a passage such as the speech of the dying Widow
Goe, while the manner of expression is abrupt and compact, the lines are managed in such a way as to emphasise the Widow's confusion of values; truth of feeling
is preserved, but the genuinely worldly and the con-
ventionally religious are *formally* sandwiched:

> 'Bless me! I die, and not a warning giv'n,—
> With *much* to do on Earth, and ALL for Heav'n!—
> No reparation for my soul's affairs,
> No leave petition'd for the barn's repairs;
> Accounts perplex'd, my interest yet unpaid,
> My mind unsettled, and my will unmade;—
> A lawyer haste, and in your way, a priest;
> And let me die in one good work at least.'

Crabbe seldom makes his uneducated characters
speak realistically. To Roger Cuff's appeal for food,
Surly John the Woodman replies:

> 'Give! am I rich? This hatchet take, and try
> Thy proper strength, nor give those limbs the lie;
> Work, feed thyself, to thine own powers appeal,
> Nor whine out woes, thine own right-hand can heal:
> And while that hand is thine and thine a leg,
> Scorn of the proud or of the base to beg'—

an answer which wins an appropriately-worded promise
of reward:

> 'Come, *surly John*, thy wealthy kinsman view,'
> Old Roger said;—'thy words are brave and true;
> Come, live with me: . . .
> Tobacco's glorious fume all day we'll share,
> With beef and brandy kill all kinds of care;
> We'll beer and biscuits on our table heap,
> And rail at rascals, till we fall asleep.'[1]

But complete realism is sometimes valuable, at least in
short snatches, as in *Peter Grimes*, when Peter beats his
apprentices and

> . . . some, on hearing cries,
> Said calmly, 'Grimes is at his exercise.'

This callously humorous understatement derives its
force from its conscious inadequacy to the occasion.

In *Tales of the Hall* Crabbe attempts a compromise
between actual educated speech and literary English;
he appears to aim at the style 'fittest for discourse and
nearest prose'. The result combines the advantages of
dramatic appropriateness and a fair measure of authenticity with the disadvantages of prolixity and stubborn
prosaism. FitzGerald, indeed, in the course of making
an abridgment of the work, and seeking to connect the
chosen extracts with 'as little of my Prose as would tell
the story of much prosaic Verse', observed that even
Crabbe's prolixity had a certain value, since 'that very
amount of prosy Verse may help to soak the story into
the mind . . . in a way that my more readable Abstract
does not'.[2] But only a reader who already liked Crabbe's
work would welcome this saturation. As for individual

---

[1] *The Parish Register*, III (*Burials*); *Works*, II, p. 228; ll. 787-9,
791-4.   [2] *Letters* (ed. Aldis Wright, 1902–3), IV, p. 57.

prosaisms, there may be different opinions on whether they are *excessively* prosaic. The classic example here is the couplet:

> And I was ask'd and authorised to go
> To seek the firm of Clutterbuck and Co.[1]

Isolated from its context, this couplet is, indeed, ludicrously flat; it cannot stand alone as can, say,

> Here, wand'ring long, amid these frowning fields,
> I sought the simple life that Nature yields.[2]

But if it is taken in its context the jar given by 'Clutterbuck and Co.' can be seen to be intentional—and also (dramatically) ironical, since the speaker is aware both of the cacophony and of the mercantile association. It is through the visit to Clutterbuck and Co. that he discovers the woman he has romantically and extravagantly loved since youth. He finds her (to quote Jeffrey) 'in a very unexpected way, and in a way that no one but Mr. Crabbe would either have thought of, or thought of describing in verse. In short, he finds her established as the *chère amie* of another respectable banker.' This, of course, we do not yet know when we read the couplet in question. But an observant reader will be aware that Crabbe does not as a rule name minor characters; the fact that this firm of bankers is named, and the choice of name, will strike him as significant. Crabbe's insistence here on his own lack of elevation should indicate that this part of the poem is one of those 'flats' from which something is soon to emerge. FitzGerald would have preferred an emendation:

[1] *The Elder Brother (Tales of the Hall*, VII); *Works*, VI, p. 150; ll. 472-3.
[2] *The Village*, I; *Works*, II, p. 78; ll. 109-10.

Might not George have spoken in character, and
defied parody, had he put it in some such way as this?
'And I was sent to put it right with—O,
Romantic Title!—Clutterbuck and Co.'[1]

This requires the poet to anticipate and insure against
adverse criticism by making patent his awareness of the
reader's probable response. But why should the reader
expect to be nudged in this way?

At the other extreme from the Elder Brother are
those uneducated characters whose utterance is more
eloquent than might seem probable. Crabbe evidently
noticed this when he was writing the story of Ruth
(*Tales of the Hall*, V). Ruth's mother tells the story with
force and fluency, especially in the final stage. The poet
appends a somewhat Wordsworthian explanation:

> Thus far the dame: the passions will dispense
> To such a wild and rapid eloquence—
> Will to the weakest mind their strength impart,
> And give the tongue the language of the heart.

A kindred explanation will suffice for the concluding
hundred lines of *Peter Grimes*. But these also show
that the language of the heart is not simply, or even
primarily, a matter of vocabulary. The taciturn Grimes,
finally made eloquent by terror, describes his hallucinations. It was when he was in his boat, 'one hot noon, all
silent, still, serene', lulled into drowsiness by watching
the running water, that his spectral persecution began:

> But dream it was not: No!—I fix'd my eyes
> On the mid stream and saw the spirits rise:
> I saw my father on the water stand,
> And hold a thin pale boy in either hand;

[1] *Readings in Crabbe, Tales of the Hall* (1882), p. 59, n.

And there they glided ghastly on the top
Of the salt flood and never touch'd a drop:
I would have struck them, but they knew th' intent,
And smiled upon the oar, and down they went.

The visitations continued; the spirits urged him to leap
to his death:

And every day, as sure as day arose,
Would these three spirits meet me ere the close;
To hear and mark them daily was my doom,
And 'Come,' they said, with weak, sad voices, 'come.'
To row away, with all my strength I tried,
But there were they, hard by me in the tide,
The three unbodied forms—and 'Come,' still 'come,'
      they cried.

Fathers should pity—but this old man shook
His hoary locks, and froze me by a look:
Thrice, when I struck them, through the water came
A hollow groan, that weaken'd all my frame:
'Father!' said I, 'have mercy:'—he replied,
I know not what—the angry spirit lied,—
'Didst thou not draw thy knife?' said he:—'Twas true,
But I had pity and my arm withdrew:
He cried for mercy, which I kindly gave,
But he has no compassion in his grave.

Finally, 'one fierce summer-day', the 'father-foe' and
the two boys appeared again, with 'more mischief in
their eyes, more glee' as they glared at him:

Still did they force me on the oar to rest,
And when they saw me fainting and oppress'd,
He, with his hand, the old man, scoop'd the flood,
And there came flame about him mix'd with blood;
He bade me stoop and look upon the place,
Then flung the hot-red liquor in my face;
Burning it blazed, and then I roar'd for pain,
I thought the demons would have turn'd my brain.

The poet has conferred on Grimes a mode of expression which harmonises with the sensations and emotions he wishes to convey. The force of the passage does not lie only in its vocabulary, but equally in its syntax and versification. Crabbe is sparing in the use of words with horrific associations (words like 'ghastly' and 'hollow groan' help to record what Grimes supposes to be the bare facts), and employs few words which are not those of common discourse; the 'weak, sad voices' and the smiles of the spirits, and their reiterated 'Come', are certainly no less horrific in effect than the hollow groans of the father's spirit. The alterations in normal word-order, as in 'dream it was not', and—even more—'He, with his hand, the old man, scoop'd the flood', make for emphasis. Further, they may be reinforced by their coincidence with an inversion of rhythm—'Thrice, when I struck them', 'Still did they force me'. There is greater flexibility of rhythm here than is usual with Crabbe, and a brilliantly used triplet and Alexandrine. It is by means of the co-ordination of elements which are not individually striking that Crabbe succeeds in rendering an impression of *habitual* terror that combines the blood-freezing and the drowsily slow.

On the merely odd, idiosyncratic, awkward or flat-footed in Crabbe's verse it seems unnecessary to dwell; it has been compendiously parodied by the authors of *Rejected Addresses*. As FitzGerald cogently observes, 'any Poetaster may improve three-fourths of the careless old Fellow's Verse: but it would puzzle a Poet to improve the better part'.[1]

[1] *Letters*, IV, pp. 67-8.

CONCLUSION

CRABBE achieved what he aimed at: the rendering of human character, in action and development, in such a way as to create clear and organised images—images which appear so closely related to actual life that, as we read the poetic fiction, the reality is as if present in the mind. For success in this endeavour two self-denying ordinances were necessary. The first consisted in making a purposeful selection look like a transcript of actuality; the second (in part a means of complying with the first) in reducing to the minimum the reader's awareness of the medium in which the poet worked. The former demanded a power of directing the reader's attention, exclusively and unremittingly, to what the poet's insight had seized upon as relevant; the latter, a mastery of forcible spareness of expression.

On the other hand, there was no self-denial in the poet's choice of material which a casual observer might think too commonplace to merit prolonged study (much less, poetic embodiment)—characters 'not discriminated by any shining or eminent peculiarities . . . which the dull overlook and the gay despise'.[1] This was the field where his interests lay; to cultivate it was a congenial task. It may perhaps be said that Crabbe's work induces a paradoxical absorption in the ordinary; but there is no evidence that he intended to do, or was aware of doing, anything paradoxical. His patient

[1] These words are from Dr. Johnson's comments on an epitaph of Pope's (*Lives of the English Poets, ed. cit.*, III, p. 262).

scrutiny resolved or transcended the paradoxes; he discerned the workings of our 'plastic nature'; and his pen not infrequently sketched them so that they compelled the mind's exclusive attention.

It is this capacity for 'possessing' the reader's consciousness by his substance without relying upon adventitious aids that is Crabbe's most striking power, rather than any ability to 'soothe and elevate the mind' (to recur to his own too general pronouncement on the proper effect of poetry). His lack of elevation has often been deplored. We may so far agree with this censure as to admit that we find *The Library* and *The Newspaper* unrewarding, and that we could easily dispense with considerable stretches of *The Borough* and with numerous tales of the order of *The Learned Boy*, *The Convert* or *'Squire Thomas*. Nevertheless, it remains true that successes like the Widow Goe or *The Frank Courtship* do not depend upon 'high hopes and aims' in any Wordsworthian sense—yet they are no less successful, in a different way, than, say, *Peter Grimes* or *Resentment* or *Sir Eustace Grey*, and they are certainly no less characteristic of their author. Indeed, Crabbe's merit is intimately connected with his not having aimed higher than 'the thing as in itself it really was', so far as he could make it out. It has been said that he had not imagination 'to draw that Soul from Nature of which he enumerates the phenomena'.[1] It might be more truly said that he refrains from giving what he does not receive from nature, and that he does not invest his chosen specimens of human nature with a significance of his own fashioning. He is suspicious of 'transport',

---

[1] FitzGerald, *Letters*, IV, p. 137. FitzGerald is here epitomising the opinion of the American critic, George Woodberry.

and eschews the factitious. He elicits only what he confidently descries, so that, at its best, his poetry creates
the impression of the work of art emerging from
nature, helped by the poet's skill in stripping away all
that is irrelevant to that particular entity.

There is obvious justice in Wordsworth's complaint
of the carelessness of Crabbe's workmanship. But still,
Crabbe's reply—'It does not matter'—shows a certain
acumen. It is true that his verbal craftsmanship is erratic
and fallible, but, oddly enough, his lapses matter less in
practice than in principle. This is partly because, since
most of his poems run to several hundred lines, the
roughnesses or mannerisms are no more than incidental
shortcomings. But the vital determining factor is that
Crabbe succeeds in envisaging his *characters-in-action* as
a whole; and the finished tale answers, so far as one can
see, to his 'idea', even though there are local slacknesses in the realisation.

A poem of any length, Coleridge assures us, neither
can, nor ought to be, all poetry. Crabbe's tales—including the best of them—are not all poetry, and it is
difficult to see how they could have been, especially in
their expositions. But they are poems. It may have been
partly an accident of literary history that Crabbe wrote
tales in verse instead of short stories. If so, it was a
happy accident. Everyday stuff, its 'commonplace'
nature not only unconcealed but, necessarily, insisted
on, is assimilated into and disclosed in a resultant poem.
Crabbe, though an imperfect poet, is an authentic and
original one. It is not that, by some sleight of hand, or
by unprecedented doggedness, he manages to drag recalcitrant material up to the lower slopes of Parnassus.
Rather, by a power of vision that can penetrate crass

surfaces, and a power of expression that can convey at once a sense of crude fact and an intimation of pervasive and meaningful process, he succeeds in conducting us through the dingy and trivial to the gradually incandescent.

INDEX

171

PRINTED IN GREAT BRITAIN
BY R. & R. CLARK, LTD., EDINBURGH